BATON TWIRLING

For the Beginner, Intermediate and Advanced Twirler

Doris Wheelus

BATON TWIRLING

A Complete Illustrated Guide

LION BOOKS · NEW YORK

This is a Lion Book
Published by Sayre Publishing, Inc.

Published in the United States by Sayre Publishing, Inc.
111 East 39 St., New York, N.Y. 10016

Library of Congress Cataloging in Publication Data

Wheelus, Doris
Baton Twirling: a complete illustrated guide

1. Baton Twirling. I Bolle, Frank. ill. II. Title
MT733.6.W5 785'.06'7108 74-22050
ISBN 0-87460-310-2
ISBN 0-87460-311-0 pbk

Manufactured in the United States of America

CONTENTS

Marching Routines - Parade Marching

Miscellaneous

Introduction

Do you want to be a majorette? You can, you know, if you have a strong enough desire to do so. All you need is this book, a baton, and the determination to be really good at it. With that, plus some hard work, concentration, and plenty of practice, you'll be out there on the football field or in a parade, marching and tossing that glittering baton with the best.

This book will teach you the Basic Fundamentals first: how to do the most essential twirls and how to march. After you've perfected those, it will show you the Advance Twirling Fundamentals and how to accomplish them. As soon as you can master them, almost without thinking, you will learn the Finger Twirls, Tricks and Novelties that will refine your style. Graceful Leaps, Aerials, Flash Series and Marching Routines come easily after earlier routines are perfected.

This book will also teach you how to organize your own Marching-Twirling group so that you can become a majorette.

So come on, girls! Study this book, buy yourself a baton, and start practicing those twirls!

How I Became a Majorette

Let me tell you how I became a majorette, and how I began to teach twirling when I was young like you. Today, as my profession, I organize and teach Twirling-Marching groups for parades of all kinds. I have four groups of wonderful, happy, hardworking girls, a total of 125 pupils all together.

More than anything else, I always wanted to be "someone"; to be "special". Most of us do, don't you think? I wanted to do something that others would admire and respect me for. I'd seen a lot of parades; I always loved to watch the bright, flashing majorettes; and one day, as I watched a high school parade, I realized that **I** could do that! I knew then and there that more than anything else, I wanted to become a majorette. And I knew I could, and would, too, some day.

When I was 13 years old, I heard that the majorette captain of our high school twirl team was teaching baton twirling for 75¢ a lesson. I talked to my best friend, Alice, who wanted to learn too, and we arranged to take lessons together.

First, our young teacher taught us the Basic Fundamentals and how to march. She kept telling us over and over to practice daily, just as seriously as if we were taking piano lessons. So each evening after school I would rush home, change into practice clothes — shorts, a sleeveless blouse or sweatshirt, and tennis shoes — and I would practice those Fundamental Twirls for one whole hour. I listed the various twirls I wanted to practice on a shorthand pad and propped it up nearby where I could glance at it now and then. I also wrote in big letters under my list, the important things to watch out for and develop. I still emphasize them to this day, and instruct each one of my pupils to write them down as I did:

- Make sure the **twirl** is correct.
- Do the twirl very slowly, making it as smooth as possible.
- Make sure your **posture** is good.
- Keep your feet close together.
- Keep the hand which isn't in use placed smartly on your waist, or a few inches below, at the point where you bend when you kick your leg out straight. Keep the **fingers** of the hand which isn't in use **close together.**
- Smile. Let your personality shine through your eyes.
- Enjoy what you are doing, even in practice.
- Lastly, work to develop **speed.**

After working on these Fundamentals, I would march all around our back yard, practicing just walking and pointing my toes down. I made sure my back was straight, leaning back just slightly, and I held my head high, as if a string were tied to the top of it, pulling it up. For several minutes, I walked and pointed my toes so that I landed on the ball of my foot. When this became easy and automatic, I began bringing my knees up higher, and higher, while keeping my marching very smooth and natural. Soon I could bring my knees up almost waist high. Then I started to practice my strut. My right hand held the baton, my left hand, fingers together, swung relaxed and naturally at my side. I practiced my smile as I marched, so that when I was in a real parade, my smile wasn't stiff and put on, but was genuine the entire time.

Nowadays, I often laugh to myself when I look back on all this. How I must have entertained our elderly next-door neighbors by marching like that all around the yard! They used to come out just to watch me. They were, I realize now, my very first audience!

Well, our teenage baton teacher soon taught us all she could, and announced we were ready for advance instruction. She made the necessary arrangements with a professional teacher and told us how to get to her house by bus. We were so thrilled to be taking advanced lessons so soon we weren't aware of how far we had to travel for those lessons.

Our new teacher had arthritis in her hands, so quite often she gave us verbal instructions without actually showing us the twirl. Right then, at that early age, I realized that some day I might be able to teach others who lived far away, just the same way, through clearly written instructions, supplemented by step-by-step drawings. I made a mental note to do just that very thing some time in the future, when I knew as much as there was to know and could do it perfectly. That is really when and where this book came into being.

Our teacher was a lovely person and she taught us a great deal more of value besides wonderful twirls and tricks. We were taught that goodness begets goodness, that a person's eyes are a reflection of the soul, that a genuine smile is contagious. Every time she smiled, we smiled. We couldn't help it.

She taught us that character and high ideals are the first important requirements of a high school majorette, and that a good majorette must be a good example to others, because she represents her school.

We tried to pass all the things she taught us on to others. For instance when our classmates smoked, Alice and I wouldn't join in with them because we felt we had an obligation to maintain our personal standards as majorettes for our school.

We had to be good students, too, to show that we could be majorettes and still keep up at least a "C" average. To prove it, each semester we had to present our report cards to the band director. Alice and I tried to maintain at least a "B" average.

Alice and I stuck with our lessons until we knew every twirl our teacher knew and she said we were letter perfect. Then it was time to try out for the high school majorette corps. Two twirlers were graduating, thus leaving two vacancies. They were sisters, the Leach twins, who were fine twirlers. Sort of for good luck, we took a private lesson from them. It proved to be a wise thing to do, because they had a lot of valuable information to give us, such as what to expect at the tryouts, what to wear, what routine twirls to demonstrate. They taught us their own special twirl, the Leach twirl, which I have included in this book. I know you will like it.

On tryout day, I was ready — but nervous. I had pressed my shorts and top with extra care, and my tennis shoes were polished snowy white.

When we walked into the room I couldn't believe my eyes. I had never seen so many girls with batons in my life. They were going to compete against Alice and me! I suddenly had a sinking sensation. I decided right off, that if I was going to win one of those spots, I would have to at least look confident, even if I didn't feel it. I kept telling this to my sweaty hands and weak knees. Our first teenage teacher had told us to tie a spoonful of baby powder or corn starch into a white hanky to dust our hands with, in just such an emergency. As were were waiting our turn, believe me, that powder dust was flying!

Finally, I heard my name called. I gave Alice a quick look, walked to the hall whispering a prayer, and began my routine by saluting the judges. I proceeded to perform as they called out the basics they wished me to demonstrate. I had worked for weeks on my routine, but I was so nervous and scared that I forgot everything completely and I just started doing the next best thing. I did every twirl I could remember, every trick I knew, whichever one that popped into my head. I smiled a lot, mostly to keep from crying. I finished my routine, almost sick with despair, and hurried back to my friend, Alice, and exploded, "I blew it, I forgot my routine. Good luck Alice, I hope you win one of the spots at least".

It seemed an eternity before the last girl returned to the room and the tryouts were over. We could see the judges gathered in a corner deliberating.

The spokesman for the judges stood. He began to talk saying, "With so much talent, it was hard to decide, but after careful consideration, we want to announce that the two new majorettes are Alice Glasby and Doris Hix". I could hardly believe my ears! I had won one spot and my best friend had won the other. It was too wonderful. I felt like laughing, like shouting . . . but all I could do was burst into tears.

I immediately called home. "Mom, I won, I won, I'm a majorette!" Her reply was, "Oh, no . . . what will that cost us?" Don't worry Mom", I said, I'll earn the money. It won't cost the family a cent." I kept that promise to my mother and paid for everything I needed to be a majorette by teaching twirling to little girls who wanted to learn. I soon had a lot of students, and was able to buy all of my costumes with plenty of money left TO PAY FOR A FIRE BATON AND A LIGHTED BATON. I saved enough that summer to go to twirling camp in Dallas, Texas, for a week as well.

I had never heard of baton twirling camp; but now the other majorettes were going to their first camp at Southern Methodist University in Dallas. It was a most exhilarating experience and an experience I will never forget. Nowadays, there are twirling camps located in all sections of the United States.

I guess that I came away from that experience in Dallas equipped to be the majorette I had dreamed of being. In addition, we were taught other things that have lived with me since, that I use today in my adult life. Furthermore, I teach my pupils the same things.

Aside from the new fresh routines that we drilled and drilled on, we came away with these concepts:

Weight Control. Nothing is pretty about a fat majorette. If you are overweight — lose. The easiest way to do that is to push yourself away from the table. You don't have to be beautiful, but you must be trim and as well groomed as possible.

Complexion Care. Keep away from fried foods and chocolate; and do not drink more than one carbonated beverage a day. Take a small amount of vitamin A daily; and, for a beautiful skin, scrub the face three times daily, especially before going to bed.

Makeup. Do not use cosmetics excessively. It is far more attractive to look natural than to look artificial. If you want to use nail polish, it should be a light shade.

Uniforms. They should always be clean and pressed.

Boots. Boots have to fit well or you will be plagued with problems. Stand when you are fitted with boots; but be certain that you have been wearing shoes for several hours when your feet will be swollen to their largest size. Powder your feet before putting on white socks under your boots. In winter, pantyhose to the waist could be worn for a nice tan look, and to protect your legs from chapping. No matter, you should always wear white socks over the hose and then put the boots on. Boots should be left to dry thoroughly after a parade to prevent bacterial foot infections.

Deodorants. A normal person's body perspires a quart a day; so if you want to keep your friends, I would suggest using a good deodorant each morning. Make sure you shower at least once a day as well.

Chewing Gum. Chewing gum during a parade or a performance is a "no-no". Nothing looks worse than a nervous gum-chewing majorette.

After learning all of this, I would think that you are now ready to start studying the pages to come. You can make baton twirling easy too . . . by starting with a bit of hard work, determination, and practice. Good luck, and great twirling!

Illustration of a Baton

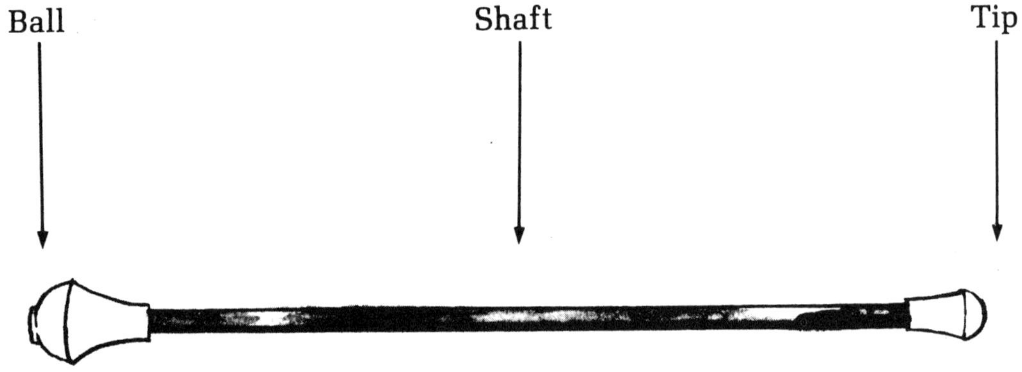

Baton Twirling

Holding the Baton

HOLDING BATON THUMB TO BALL

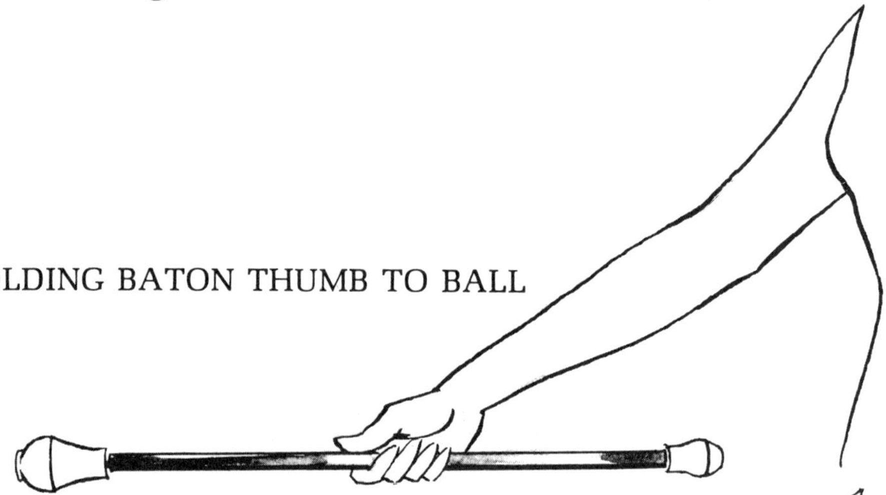

HOLDING BATON THUMB TO TIP

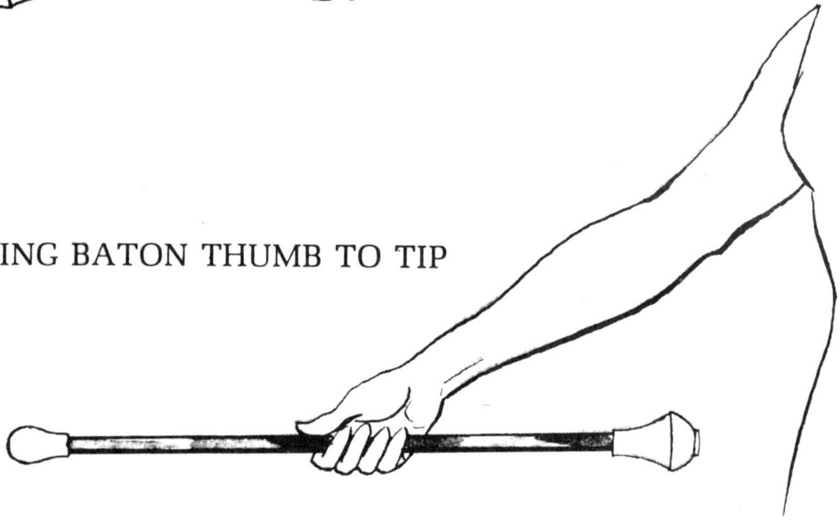

HOLDING BATON IN CENTER OF SHAFT

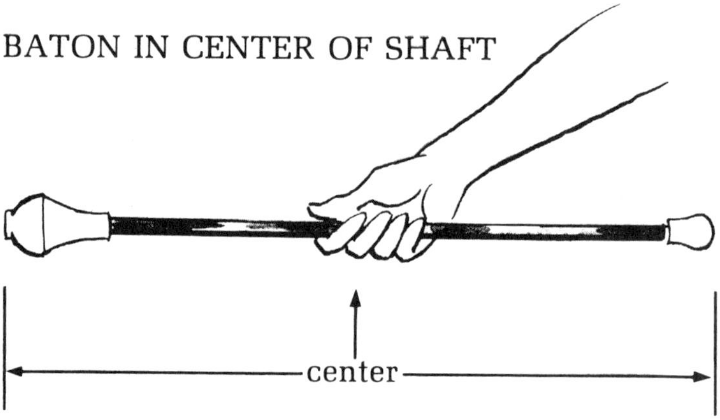

How to March

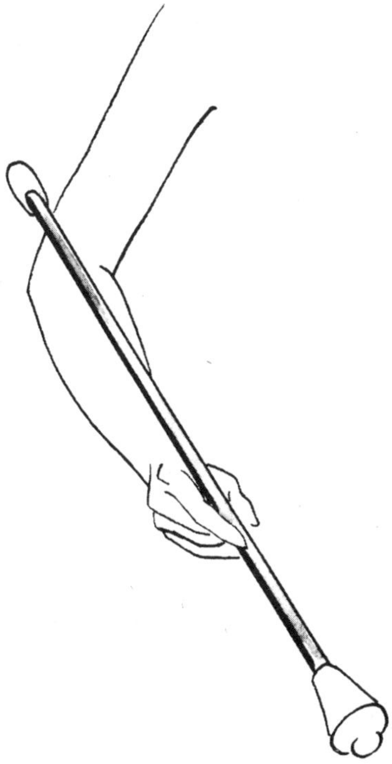

1. Stand tall, back straight, shoulders back, head high.

2. Now imagine that your baton is a jumbo-size pencil. Hold it as you would hold a pencil when writing. The ball of the baton should be toward the ground. (See illustration 1)

3. Start out with your left foot. Practice walking with your toes pointed towards the ground. As this becomes natural, start bringing your knees up higher still. The ball of your foot should touch the ground first, rather than your heel. (See illustration 2)

4. Your left hand will swing at your side very naturally, but be sure to keep your fingers together. The swing of your baton and the swing of your left hand will come to you very naturally as you practice your marching.

BASIC TWIRLING FUNDAMENTALS

Horizontal Twirl–Right Hand

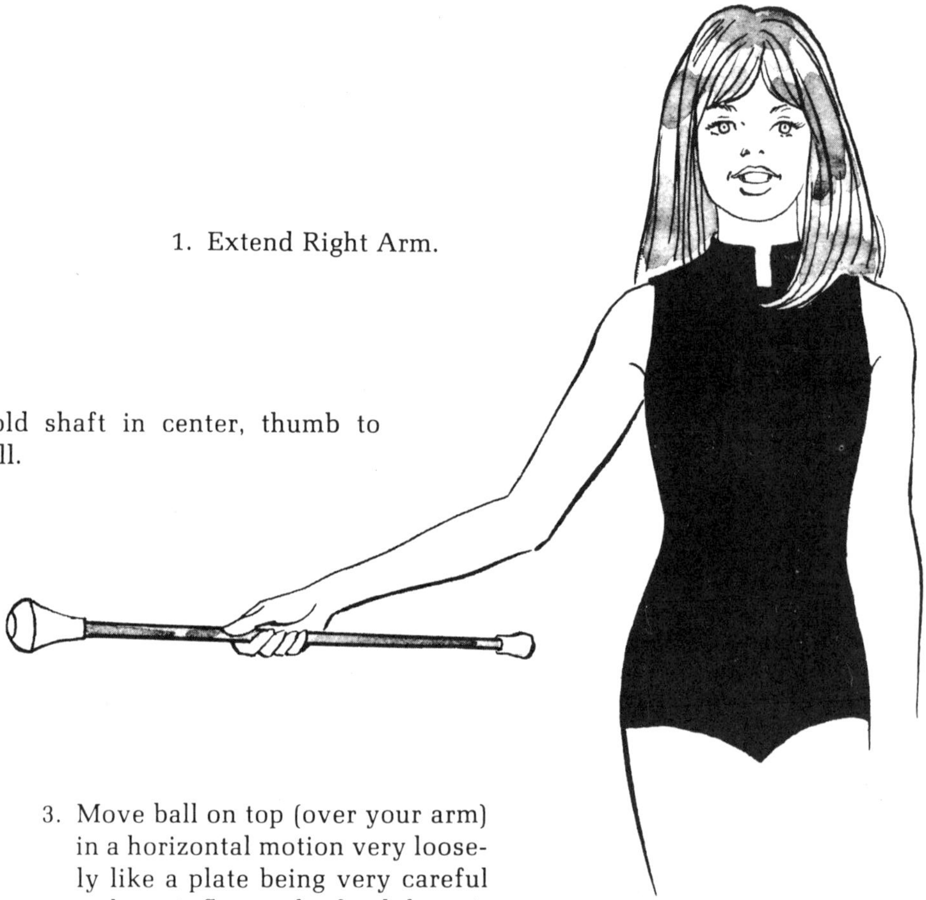

1. Extend Right Arm.

2. Hold shaft in center, thumb to ball.

3. Move ball on top (over your arm) in a horizontal motion very loosely like a plate being very careful to keep it flat so the food doesn't fall off the plate. The tip of the baton will be on bottom (under your arm).

Horizontal Twirl–Left Hand

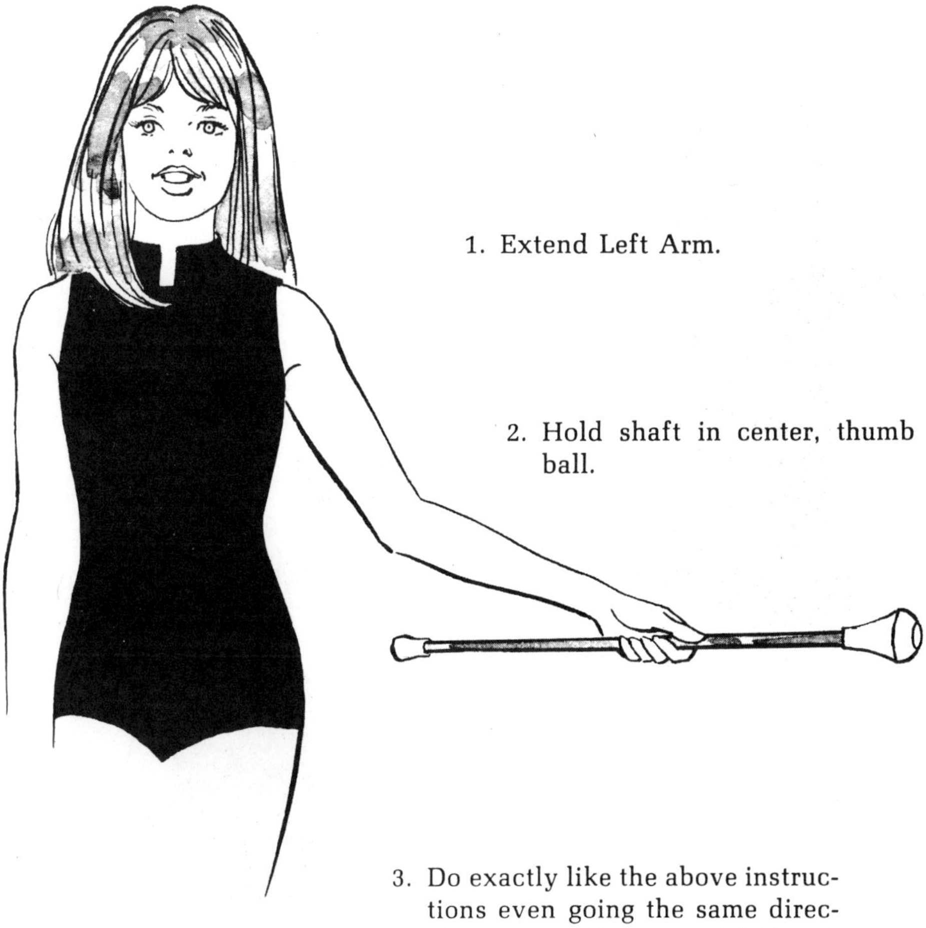

1. Extend Left Arm.

2. Hold shaft in center, thumb to ball.

3. Do exactly like the above instructions even going the same direction as you did in your right hand.

Horizontal Twirl–
Pass from Right Hand to Left

1. Do horizontal twirl in right hand and while continuing this twirl very slowly put left hand thumb and index finger around baton forming an O.

2. Then take in left hand going in the same direction as you were in the right hand. This is a simple way to check to make sure your direction of your baton is correct. Your twirl in your right hand is the very same direction when you put it in your left hand.

3. Try to keep your horizontal twirl in your left hand flat as a plate.

Horizontal Twirl-Toss to Right Hand

1. You are doing horizontal in left hand so give a little toss upward just high enough to keep your horizontal motion going and enough to get it over to your right hand and catch with right hand.

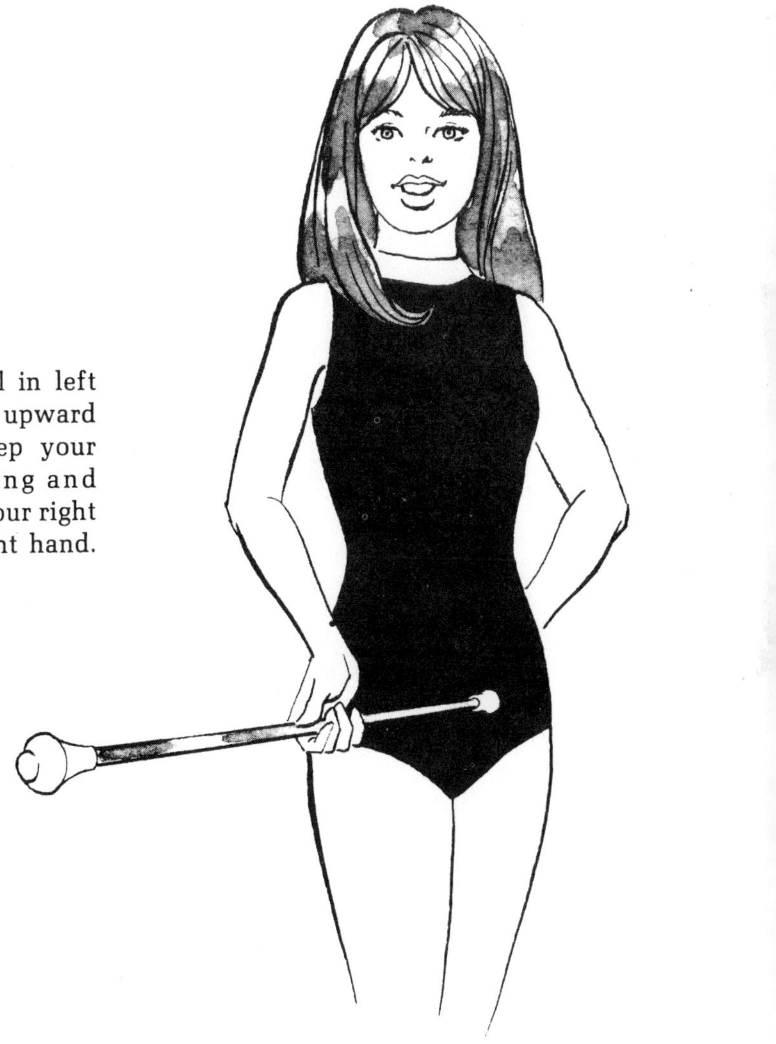

Wrist Twirl-Right Hand

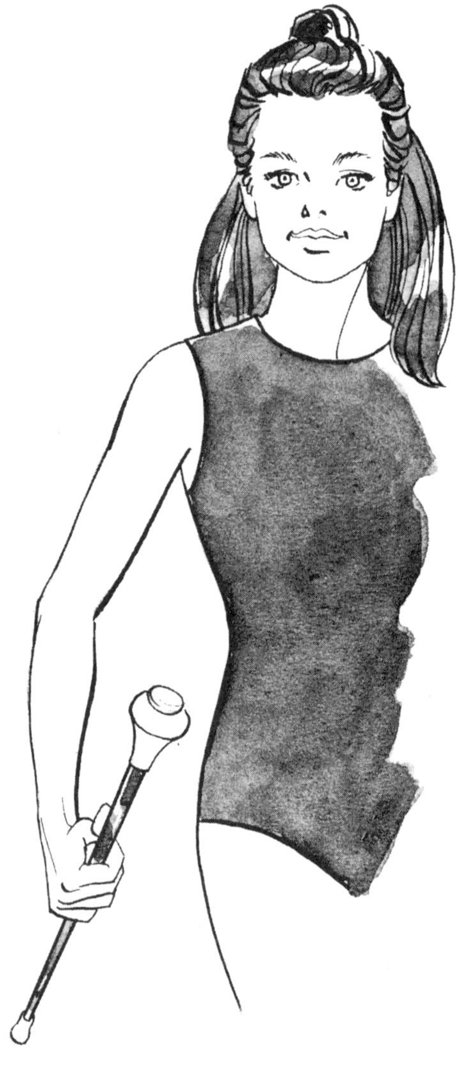

1. Arm straight down to your side, hold baton in middle of shaft, thumb to ball.
2. Turn the baton so that the ball moves forward and downward in vertical, circular motion using a very loose wrist.
3. The ball of the baton should go on the inside of your arm every time and the tip should go on the outside of your arm.

Note: Practice this twirl feet together, back straight, head high, left hand on waist, thumb behind, fingers together.

Wrist Twirl–Left Hand

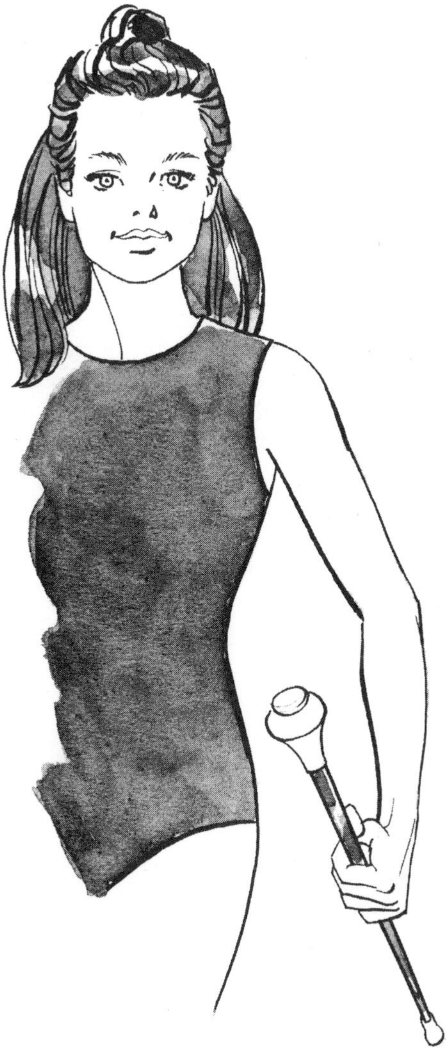

1. Do same as right hand but baton will be in left hand. Hold baton in middle of shaft, thumb to ball. Ball of the baton will go on the inside of your arm every time and the tip on the outside.

Note: Practice this twirl feet together, back straight, head high, right hand on waist, thumb behind, fingers together.

Figure 8 – Right Hand

1. Hold baton in right hand, thumb to ball.

2. Pretend there is a can of paint in front of you. Pretend you are dipping the ball of the baton in the can of paint.

3. Dip (Illustration 1), turn your hand over (down) (Illustration 2) Dip (Illustration 3) . . . Begin again . . . Do several times.

Illus. 1

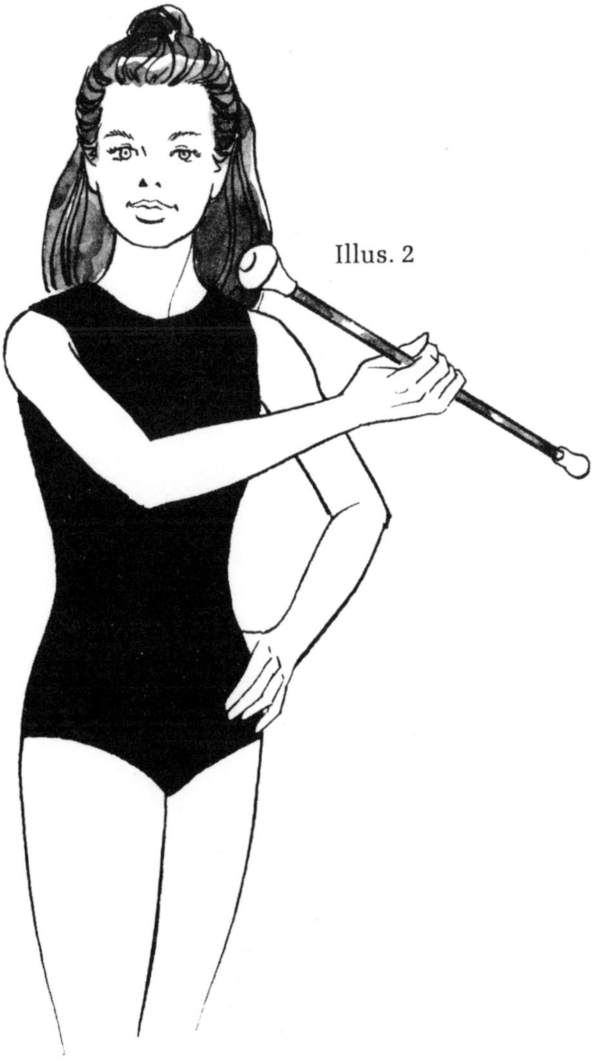

Illus. 2

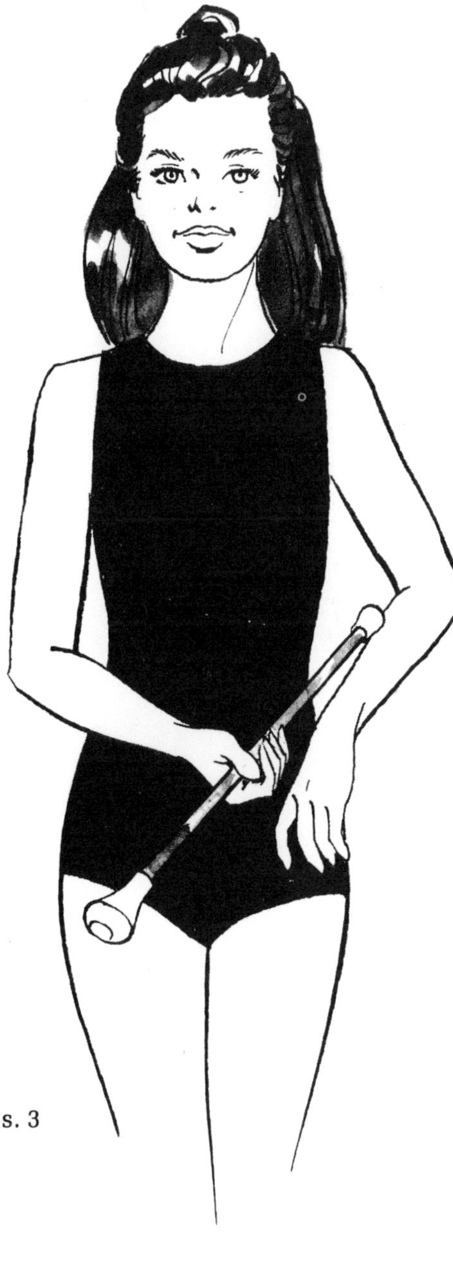

Illus. 3

Figure 8-Left Hand

1. Hold baton in left hand, thumb to ball.

2. Do exactly like the instructions for Figure 8—Right Hand.

Forward Inside Circle

1. Hold baton out to side of body, deep between the thumb and forefinger. (See illustration.)

2. To start twirl, drop the ball away from the body and down making one single circle. The ball should always pass inside the elbow and the tip should always pass outside the elbow.

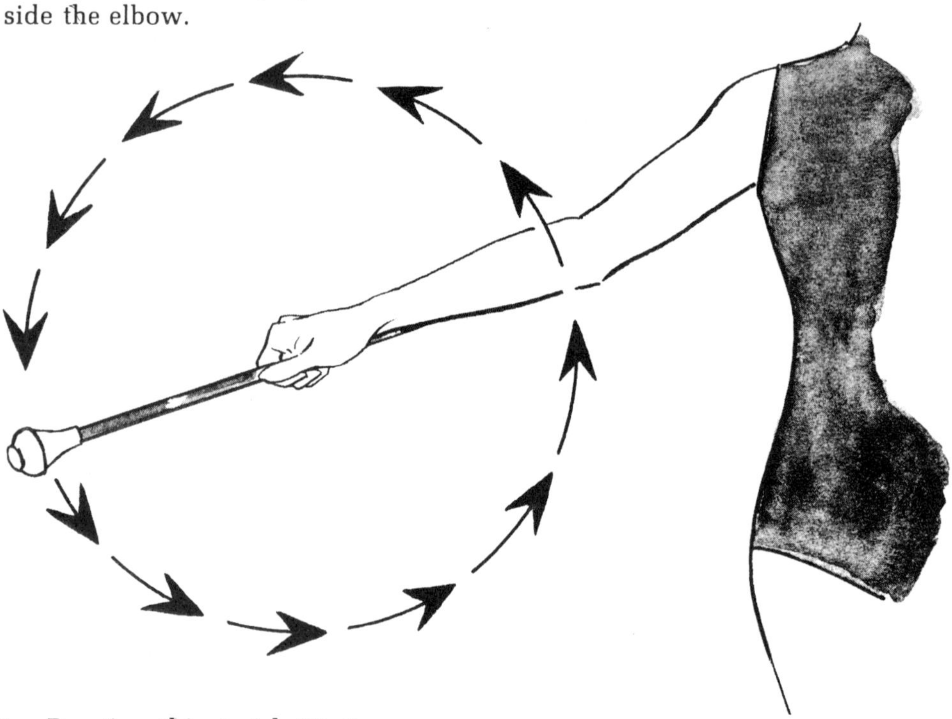

Note: Practice this twirl 20 times making 20 complete circles. Say the name of the twirl as you do it, "Forward Inside Circle". This twirl will be used often in your more advanced twirls.

Backward Inside Circle

1. Hold baton in middle of shaft, thumb to ball. Bring the ball of the baton towards the body making a reverse single circle. The ball will always pass on the inside of the elbow and the tip will always pass on the outside of the elbow.

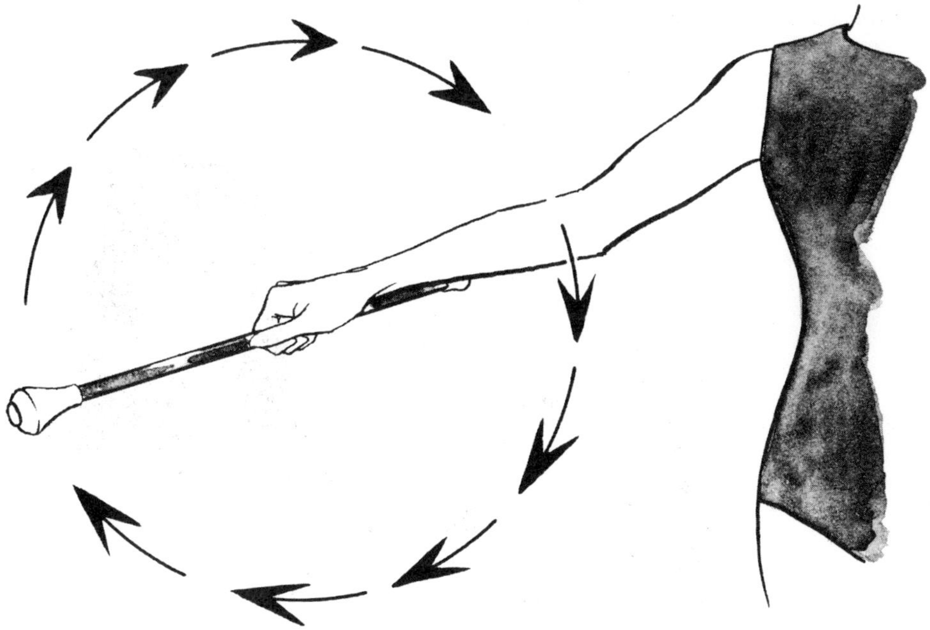

Note: Practice this twirl 20 times making 20 complete circles. Say the name of the twirl as you do it, "Backward Inside Circle". This twirl will be used often in your more advanced twirls.

Forward Outside Circle

1. Hold baton to side of body, thumb to ball. (See Illustration 1)

2. To start twirl, the ball of the baton should move away from the body and down making a vertical circle at the side of the body. The ball should always pass outside the elbow and the tip circles inside the elbow.

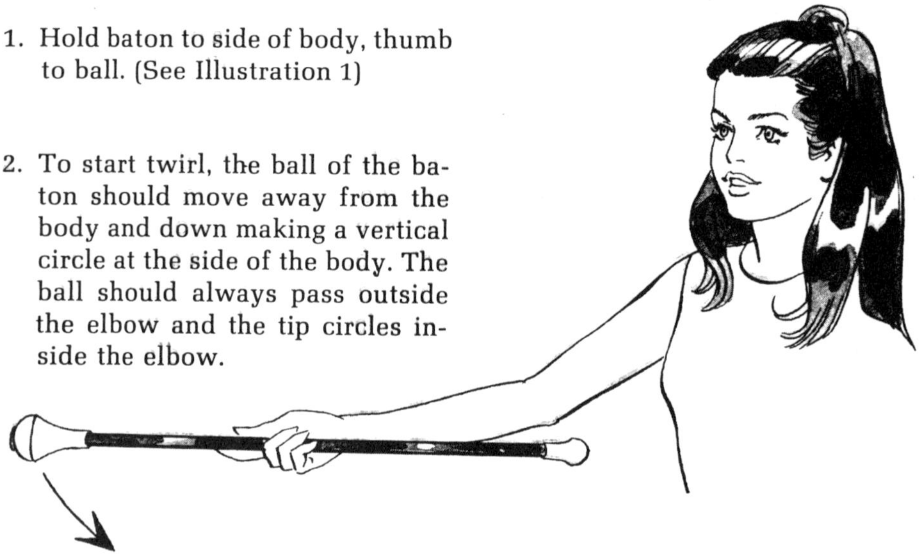

Illus. 1

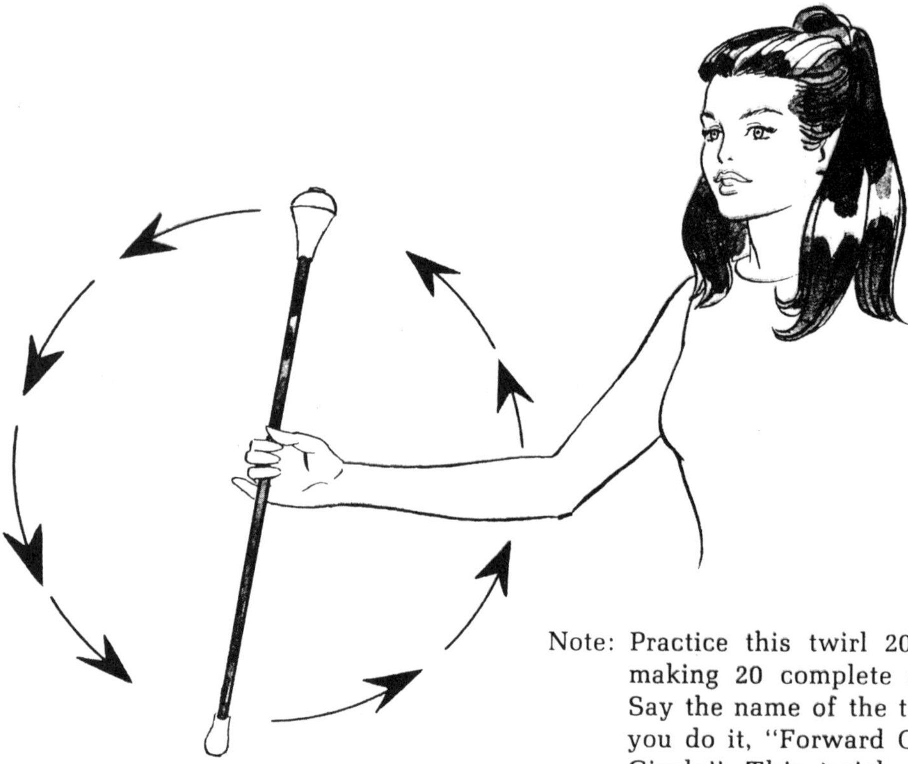

Note: Practice this twirl 20 times making 20 complete circles. Say the name of the twirl as you do it, "Forward Outside Circle". This twirl will be used often in your more advanced twirls.

Backward Outside Circle

1. Hold baton to side of body, thumb to ball. (See Illustration 1)

Illus. 1

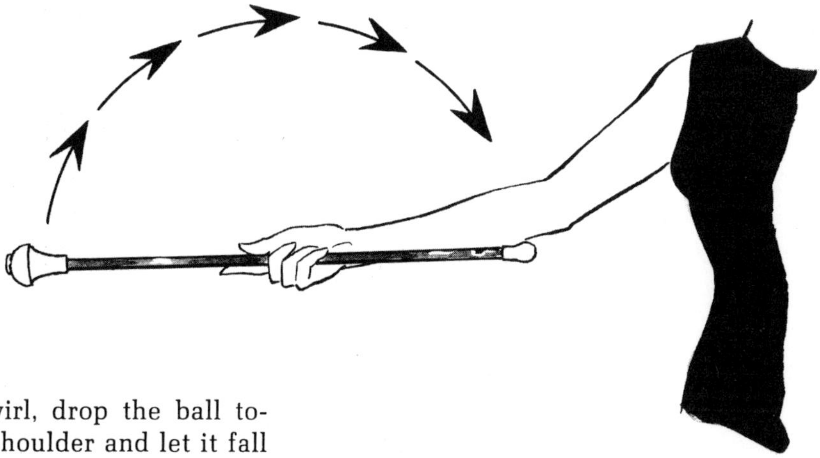

2. To start twirl, drop the ball towards the shoulder and let it fall to the outside of the elbow in a reverse motion. (See Illustration 2) *(The ball always passes on the outside of the elbow and the tip always passes on the inside of the elbow.)* Make one complete circle. Your position of your hand and baton will be the same as Illustration 1 when you are finished.

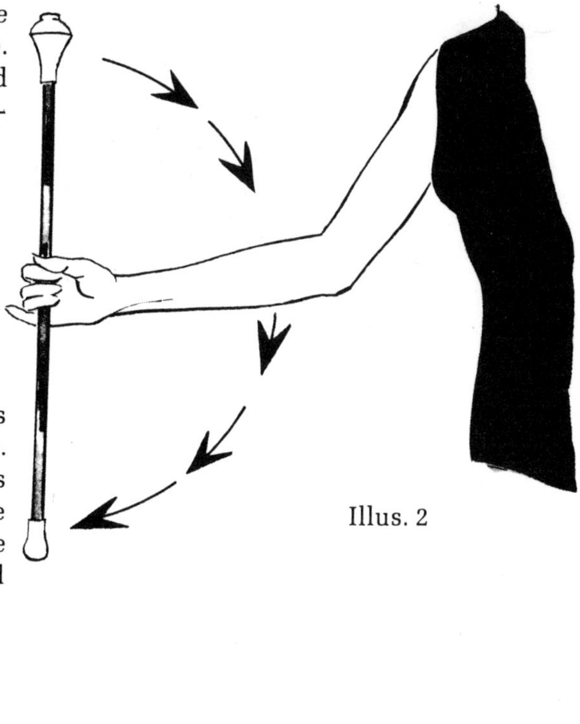

Illus. 2

Note: Practice this twirl 20 times making 20 complete circles. Say the name of the twirl as you do it, "Backward Outside Circle". This twirl will also be useful in your more advanced twirls.

Front Two Hand Spin

1. Hold baton in right hand—thumb to tip, ball of the baton to the right. (Illustration 1).

2. Turn baton over. (Illustration 2).

3. Lay left hand on top of baton, palm up. (Illustration 3).

Illus. 1

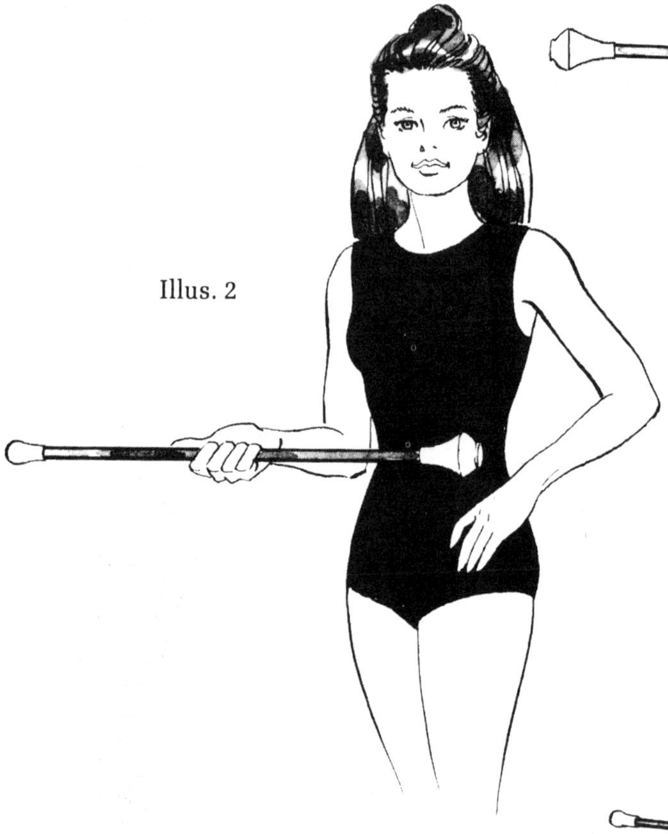

Illus. 2

Illus. 3

4. Hook left hand thumb under shaft.

5. Let baton go into left hand. (Illustration 4).

6. Turn baton over, left hand knuckles up. (Illustration 5).

7. Put right hand beside it, knuckles up. (Illustration 6).

8. Remove left hand from baton.

9. Start all over again . . .

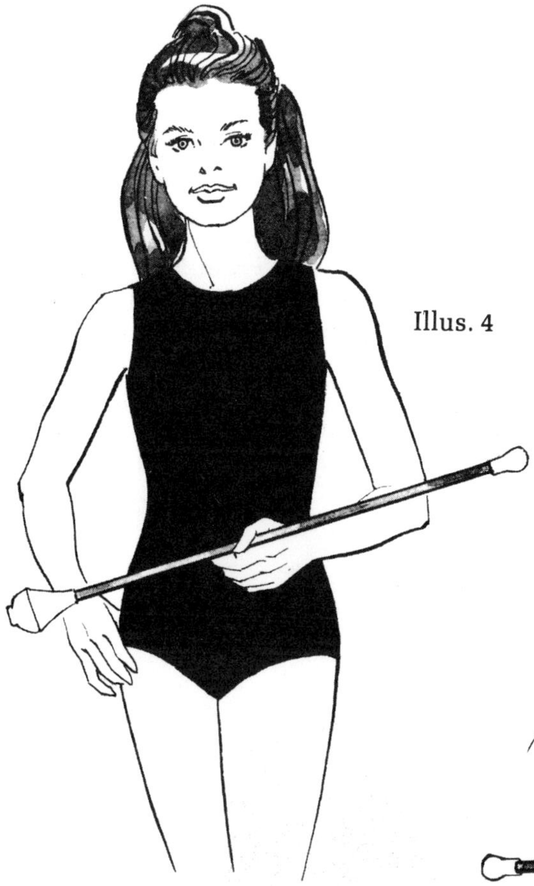

Illus. 4

Illus. 5

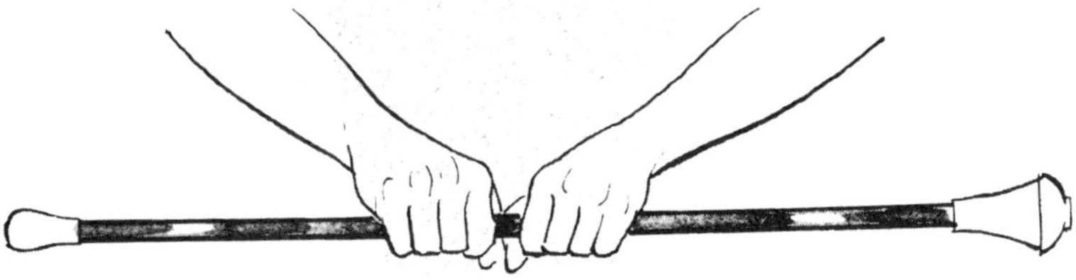

Illus. 6

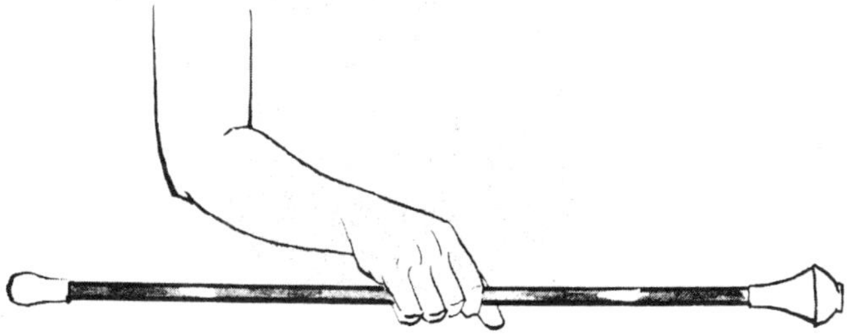

Illus. 7

Front Two Hand Spin - Pass Around Waist

1. Begin the Front Two Hand Spin. When the baton is in the left hand (Illustration 1), pass around waist to right hand (Illustration 2). You may now go to another fundamental twirl or trick or you may continue your Front Two Hand Spin.

Illus. 1

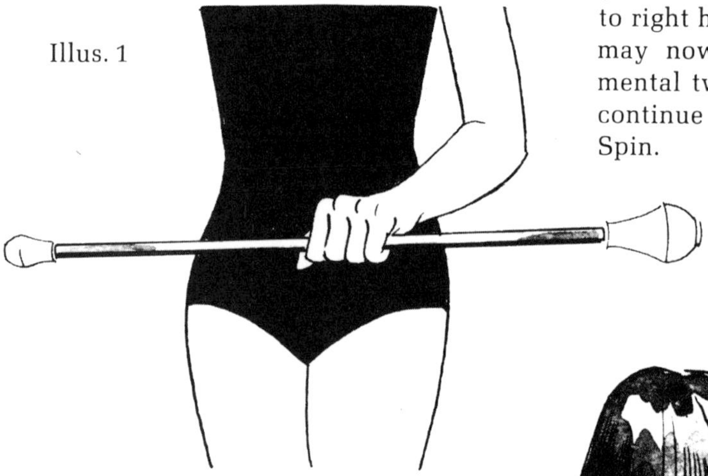

Helpful Hints: The natural follow-up of the Front Two Hand Spin is the Pass Around Waist. These two movements are used often to get from one twirl to another smoothly without a break in the continuity of the spinning motion.

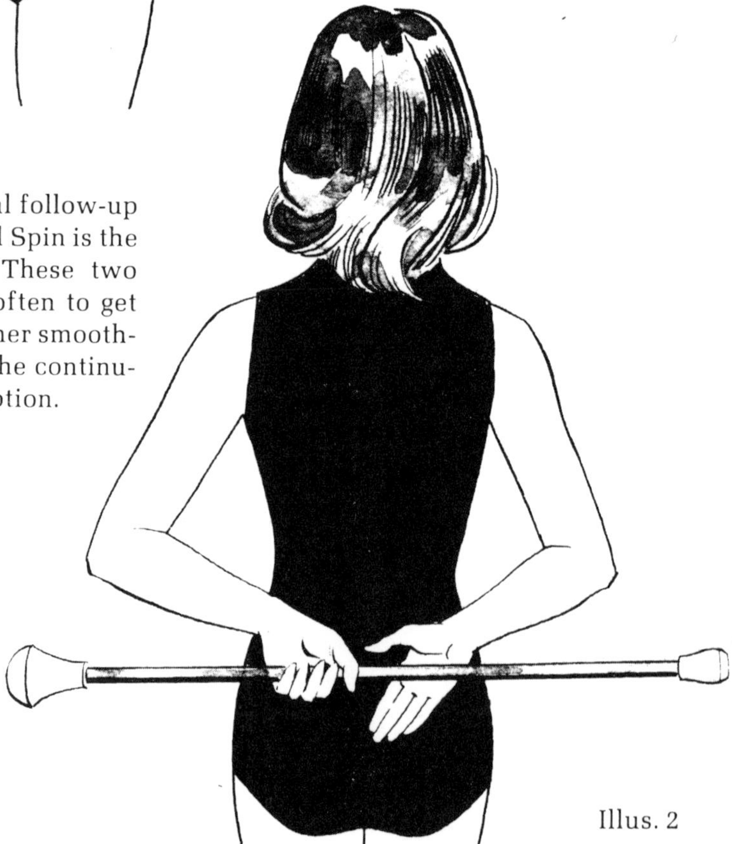

Illus. 2

Front Two Hand Spin – Pass Around Knees

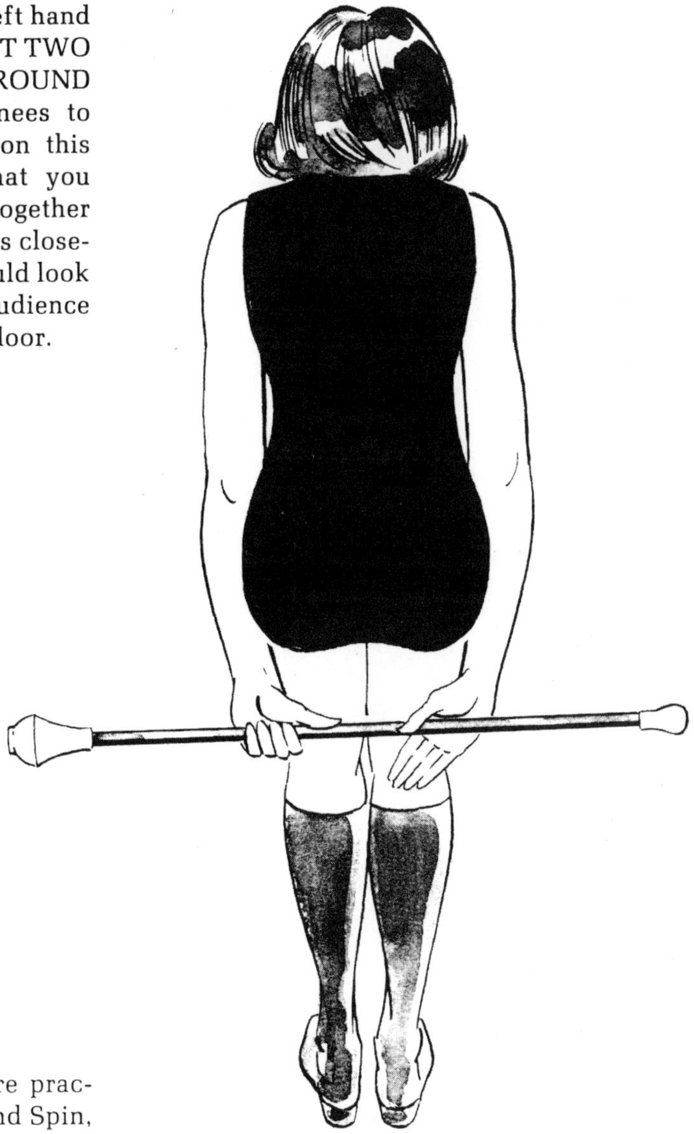

1. Begin the Front Two Hand Spin. When the baton is in the left hand (See Illustration 1—FRONT TWO HAND SPIN — PASS AROUND WAIST), pass around knees to right hand (See illustration this page). It is important that you keep your feet closely together and to also keep your knees closely together. Your face should look straight out as if at an audience rather than down to the floor.

Helpful Hints: While you are practising your Front Two Hand Spin, practice your pass around waist and pass around knees.

Front Wheel–Right Hand

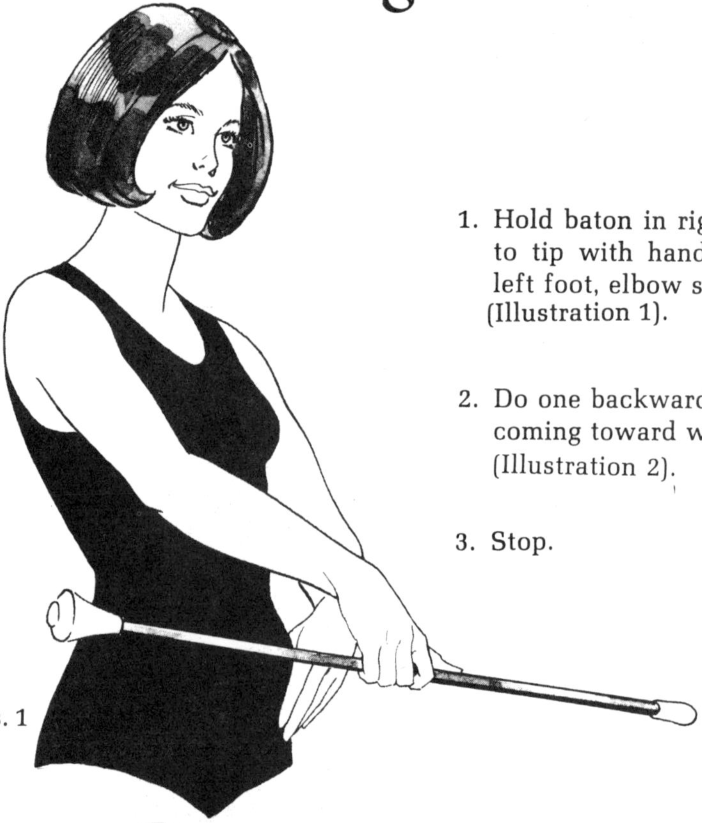

Illus. 1

1. Hold baton in right hand, thumb to tip with hand directly above left foot, elbow straight. (Illustration 1).

2. Do one backward wrist twirl (tip coming toward waist). (Illustration 2).

3. Stop.

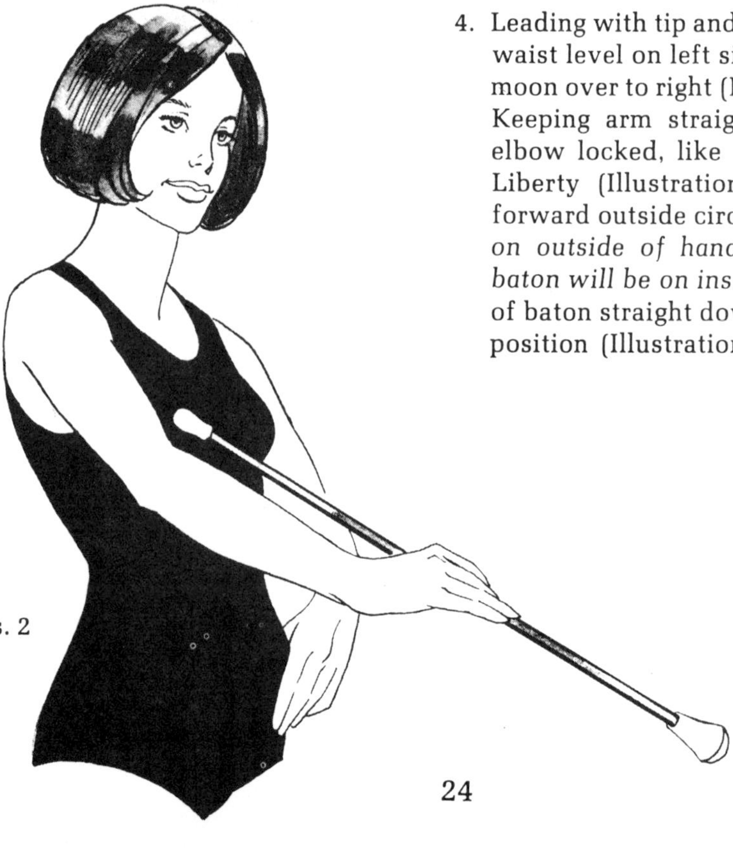

Illus. 2

4. Leading with tip and starting from waist level on left side, draw half moon over to right (Illustration 3). Keeping arm straight up in air, elbow locked, like the Statue of Liberty (Illustration 4). Do one forward outside circle *(tip will be on outside of hand and ball of baton will be on inside)*. Bring tip of baton straight down to starting position (Illustration 5).

5. Begin again.

6. Do several times.

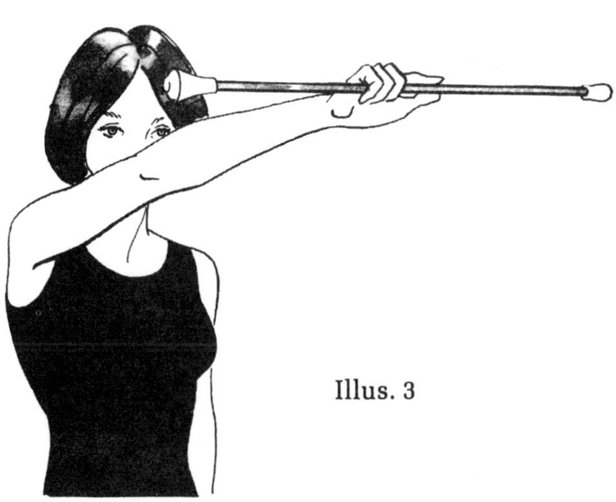

Illus. 3

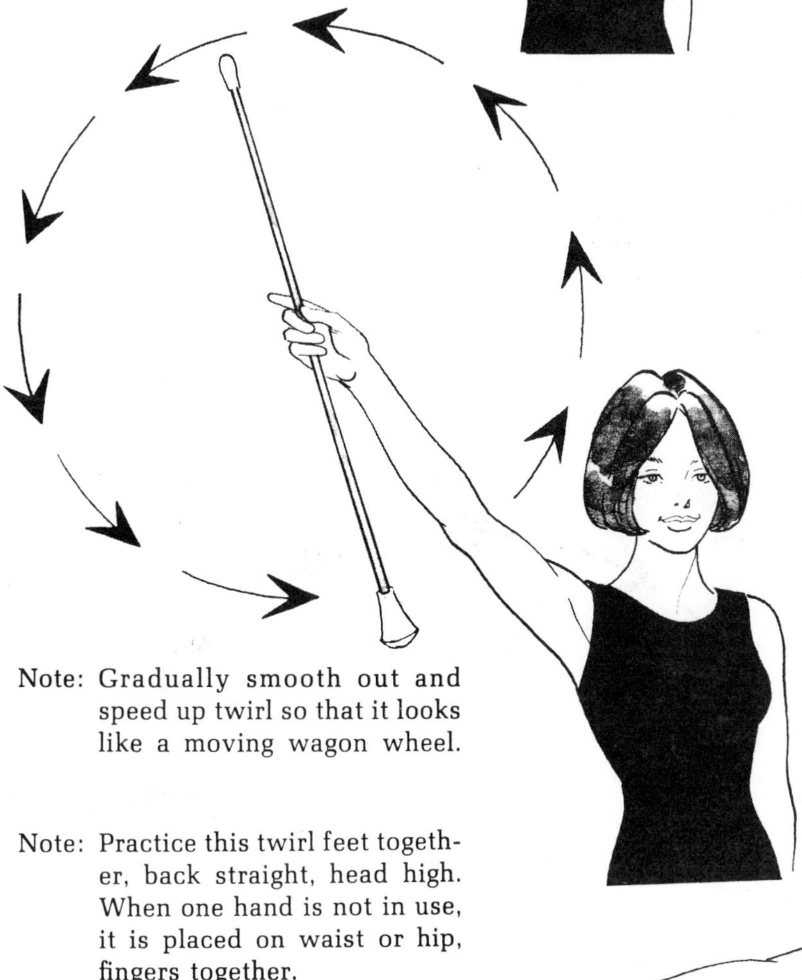

Illus. 4

Note: Gradually smooth out and speed up twirl so that it looks like a moving wagon wheel.

Note: Practice this twirl feet together, back straight, head high. When one hand is not in use, it is placed on waist or hip, fingers together.

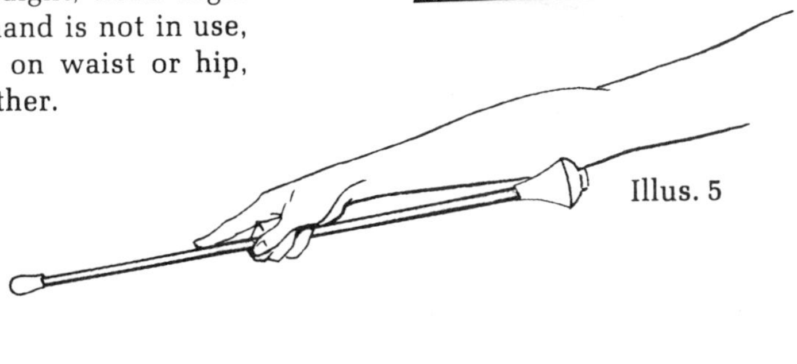

Illus. 5

Time Toss

1. Hold baton in right hand (waist high) thumb to tip, knuckles will be up.

2. Turn hand over quickly (palm will be open) tip going to the right.

3. Push upward off thumb.

4. Baton should make one complete revolution or circle when twirl is mastered. Catch thumb to tip in right hand.

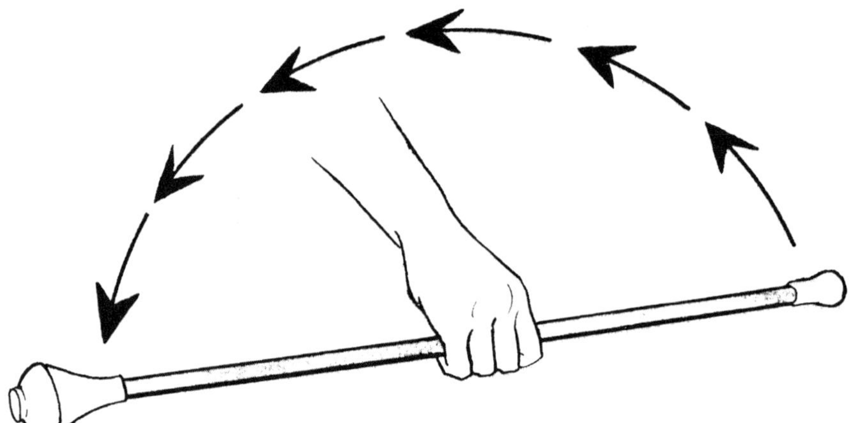

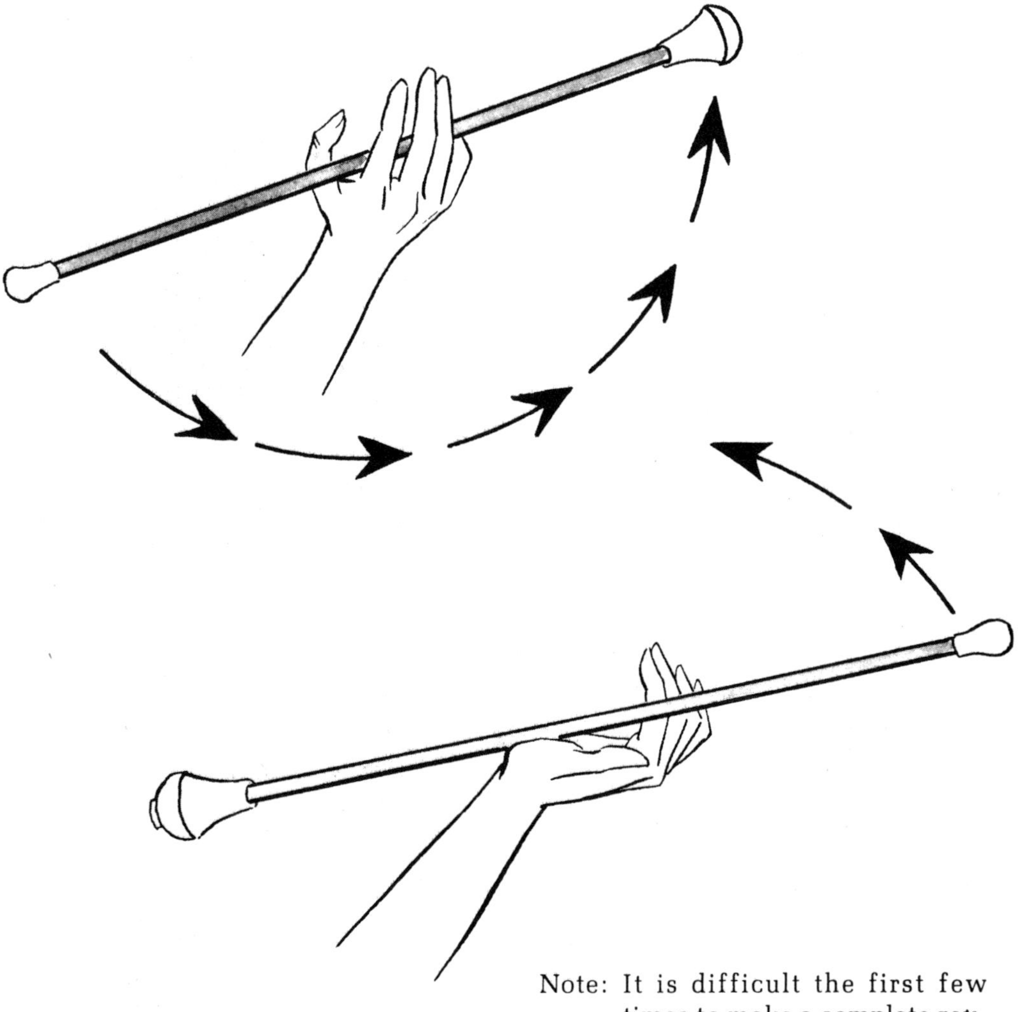

Note: It is difficult the first few times to make a complete revolution and catch your baton as you should (thumb to tip). It will take many hours of practice. When you master one revolution and catch your baton correctly increase your revolutions to 5, then 10, then 20 and on and on. Practice this twirl feet together, shoulders back, head high, left hand on waist, thumb behind, fingers together.

Twirl Around The Body

1. Hold the baton in right hand, thumb to ball. Put left hand on hip. Do one Figure Eight at side. (Illustration 1)

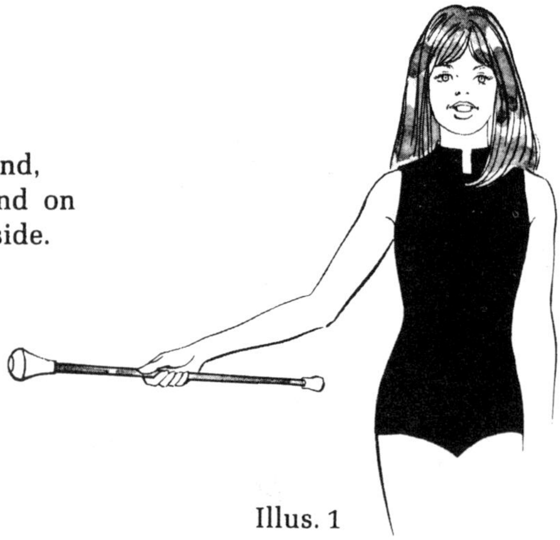

Illus. 1

Illus. 2

2. Dip the ball of the baton in back of the body, waist high. Left hand reaches behind the body to take hold of the shaft in the center, thumb to tip, palms turning out, away from body. (Illustration 2).

3. Right hand releases hold on shaft and is placed on right hip. (Illustration 3).

4. Baton is extended straight out on left side. Do one backwards outside circle. (Circle with the tip of the baton on the outside of your arm. (Illustration 4).

5. Leading with the tip of the baton, bring the baton high in front of the body in a horizontal position over the head. The right hand grasps the shaft, thumb to ball.

6. Remove left hand.

Illus. 3

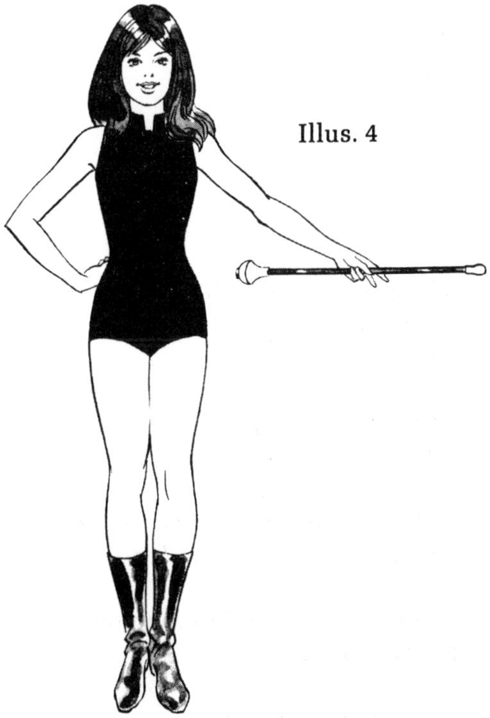

Illus. 4

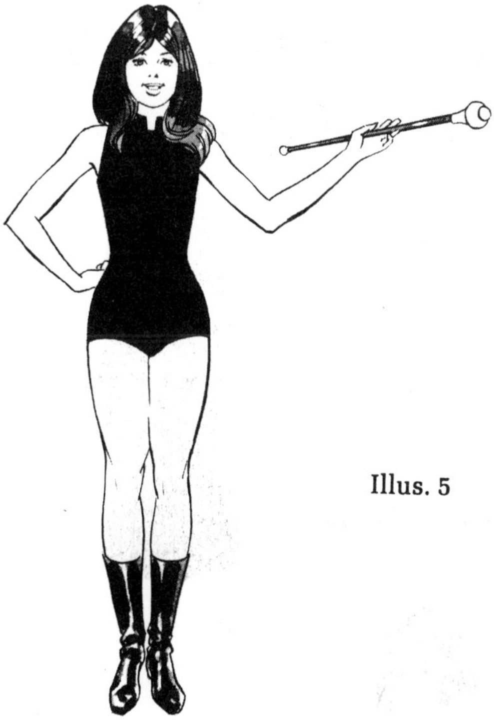

Illus. 5

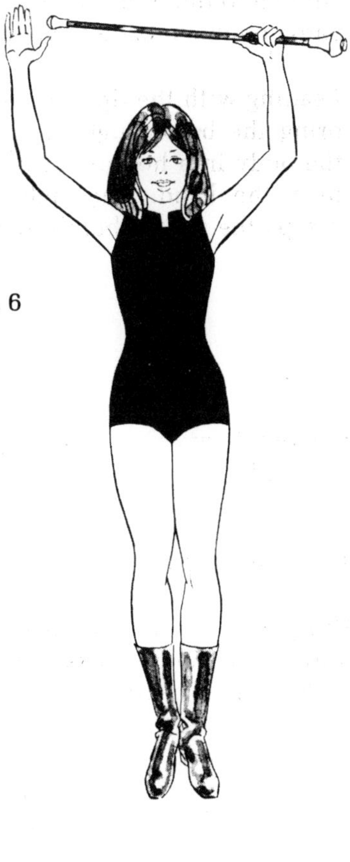

Illus. 6

7. Bring the tip of the baton straight down in a vertical position, ball on top, tip on bottom to right side.

8. To repeat twirl, begin Figure Eight again . . .

Illus. 7

Twirl Around The Body - Under Legs

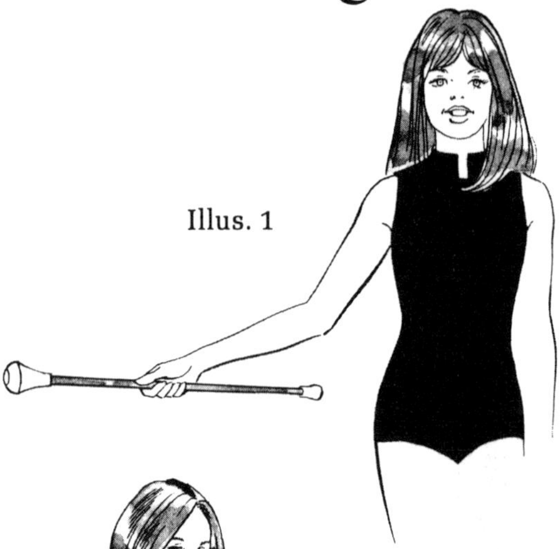

Illus. 1

1. Hold baton in right hand, thumb to ball. Do one Figure Eight at side.

2. Raise right leg up waist level, point toe downward.

3. Leading with ball of the baton, bring baton under right leg.

4. Take hold of baton, thumb pointing towards the tip.

5. Extend baton straight out on left side. Do one backwards outside circle (circling with the tip of the baton on the outside of your arm).

6. Leading with the tip of the baton, bring the baton high in front of the body in a horizontal position over the head. The right hand grasps the shaft, thumb to ball.

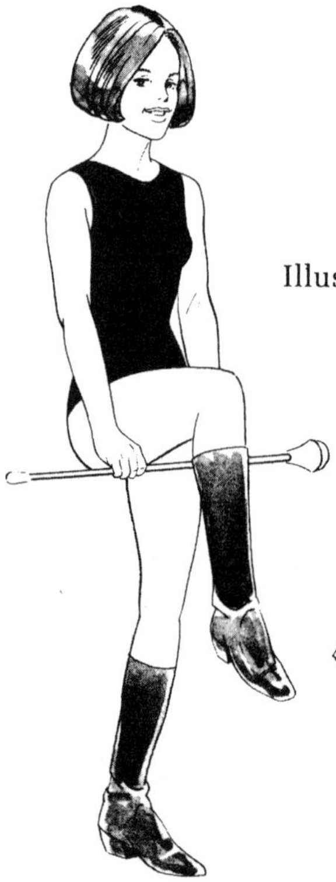

Illus. 2

Illus. 3

7. Remove left hand.

8. Bring the tip of the baton straight down in a vertical position, ball on top, tip on bottom.

Illus. 4

Illus. 5

Illus. 6

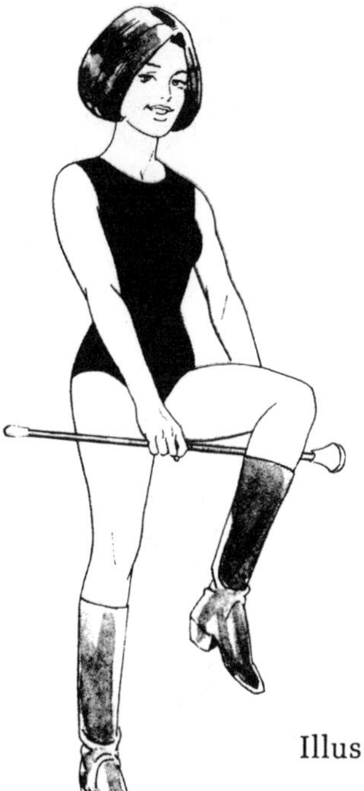

Illus. 7

9. Raise the left leg waist level toe pointed downward.

10. Do one Figure Eight, leading with ball, bring baton under left leg and repeat same procedure . . .

Reverse

1. Hold baton thumb to ball. (Illustration 1)

2. Draw a circle, ball going under your arm.

3. Do a Front Two Hand Spin in front. Take in your left hand. (Illustration 2)

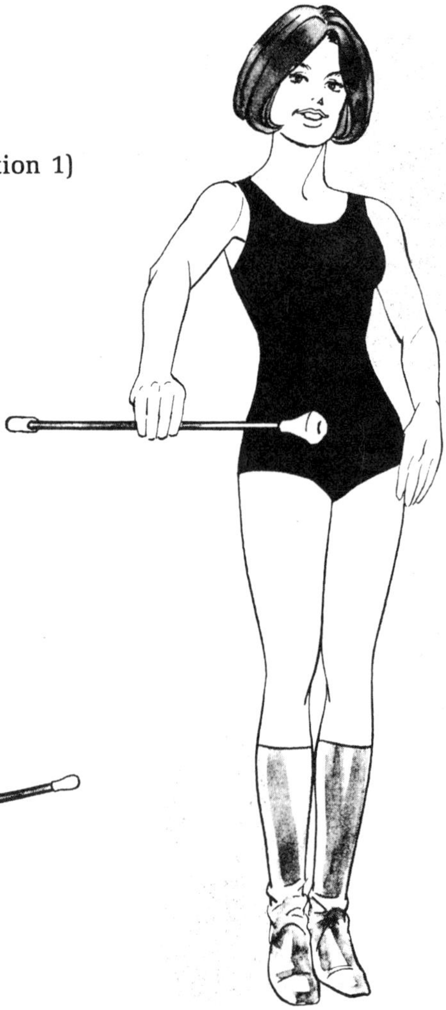

Illus. 2

4. In your left hand do a backwards outside circle at your left side. (Illustration 3)

5. Pass in front. (Illustration 4)

6. Take in right hand and do a forward outside circle at your right side. (Illustration 5)

Illus. 3

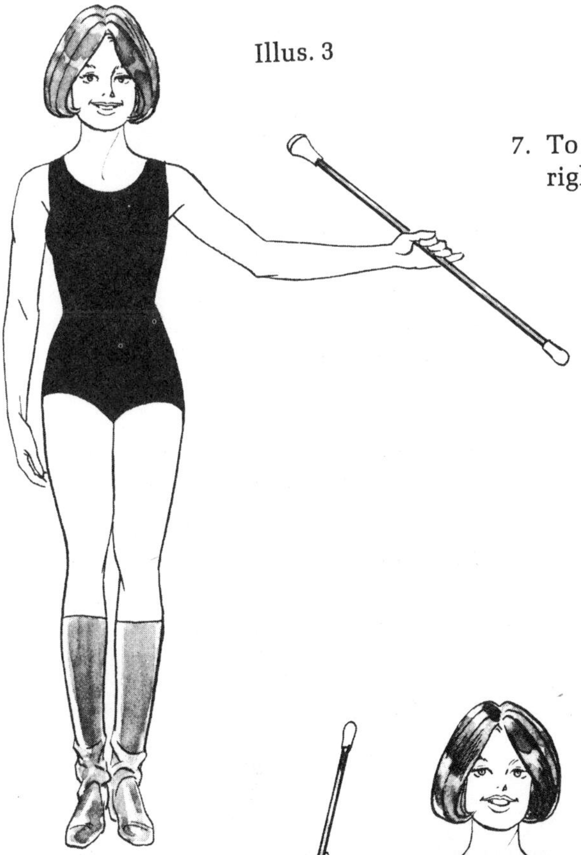

7. To repeat twirl, draw circle under right arm . . .

Illus. 4

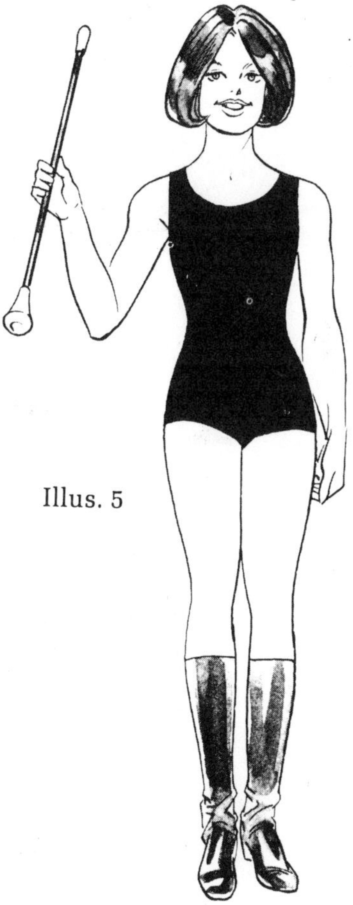

Illus. 5

Double Reverse

1. Hold baton in right hand, thumb to ball, put left hand on hip. Do one Figure Eight at side.

2. Dip the ball in back of the body, waist high. Left hand reaches behind the body to take hold of the shaft in the center, thumb to tip, palms turning out, away from body.

3. Right hand releases hold on shaft and is placed on right hip.

Note: Steps 1, 2 and 3 are the same as Steps 1, 2 and 3 in Twirl around Body twirl.

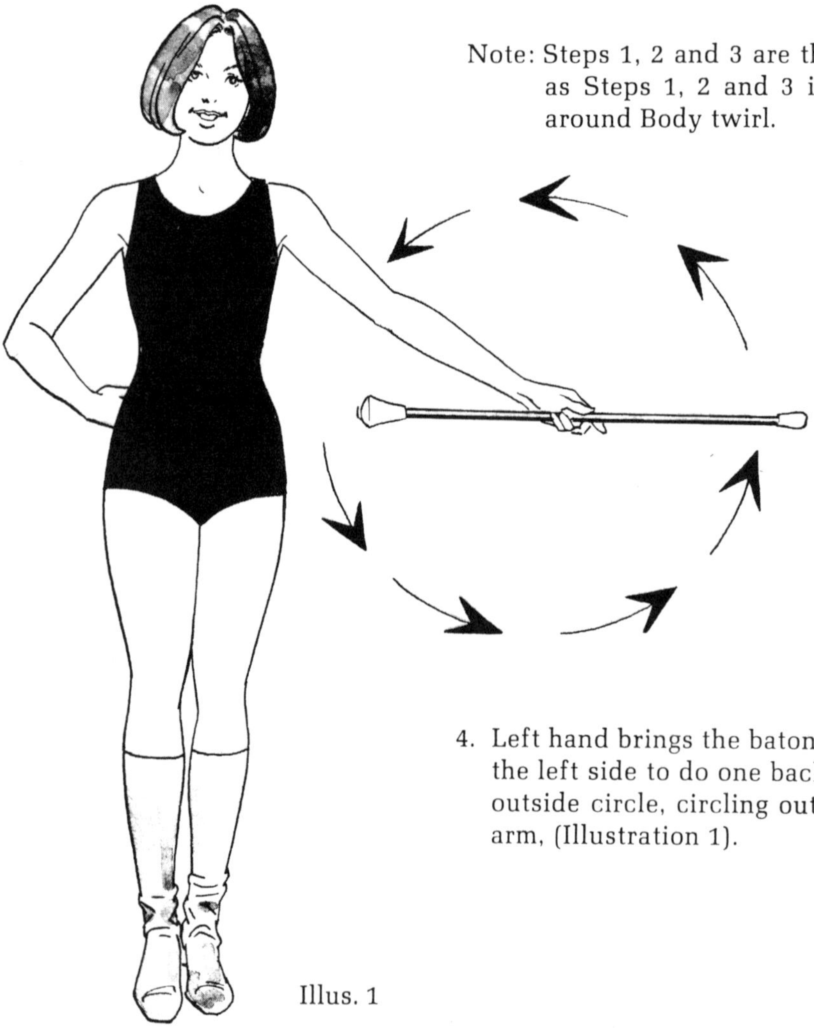

4. Left hand brings the baton out on the left side to do one backwards outside circle, circling outside of arm, (Illustration 1).

Illus. 1

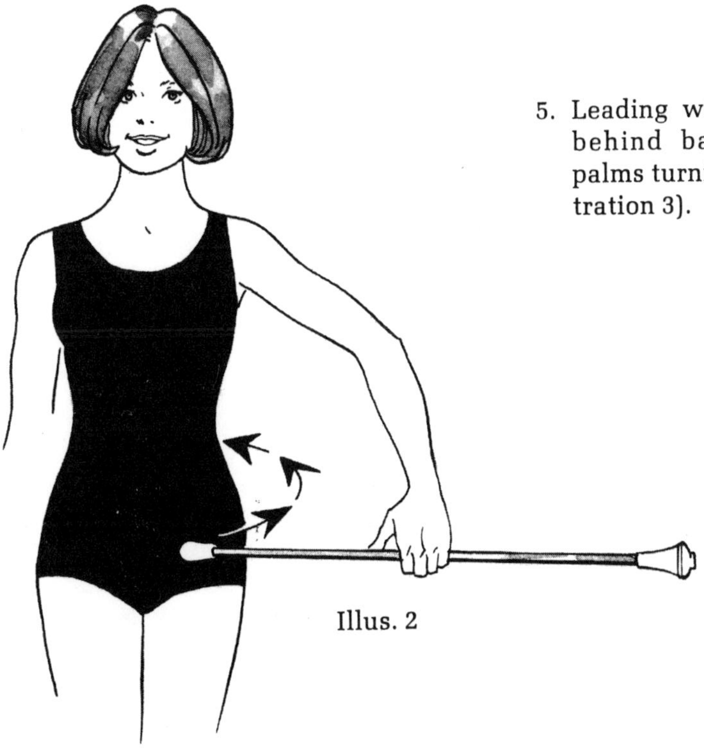

Illus. 2

5. Leading with tip of baton, pass behind back, (Illustration 2), palms turning outward. (See illustration 3).

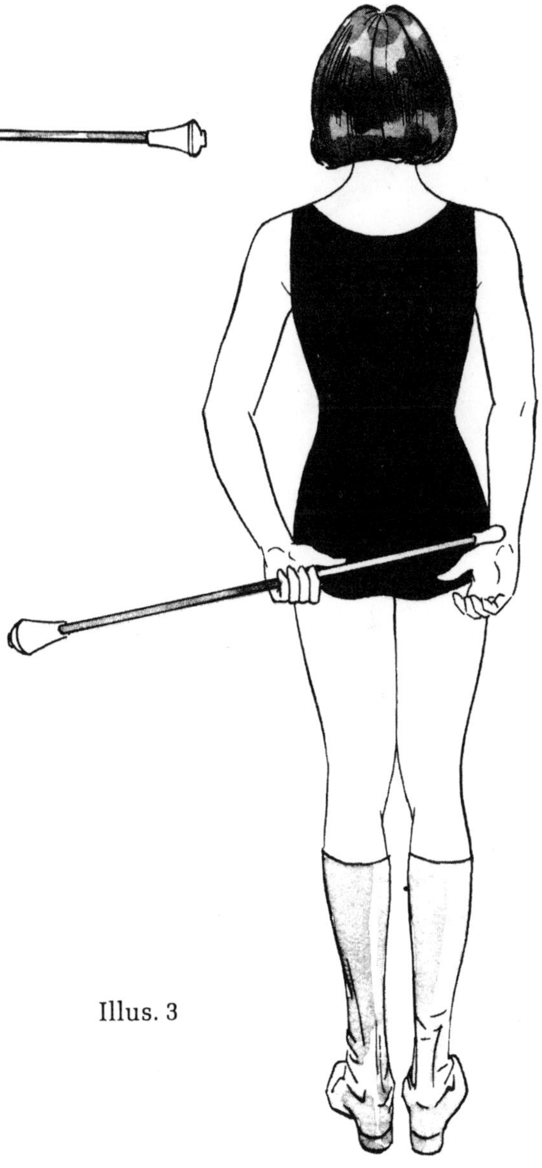

Illus. 3

6. Behind back take baton in right hand, thumb to ball, (Illustration 3).

7. Release left hand and place on hip.

8. Bring right hand and baton from behind back to right side to begin twirl again by doing one Figure Eight at side.

Cartwheel

Illus. 1

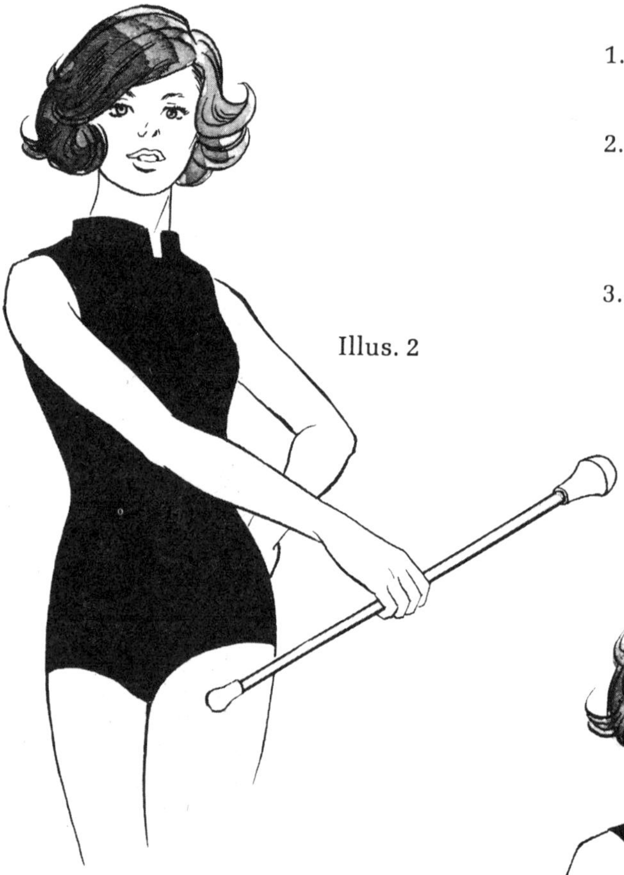

Illus. 2

1. Hold baton in right hand, thumb to ball. (See Illustration 1)
2. Leading with ball of baton, dip across body to left side as if to do a Figure Eight. (See Illustrations 2 and 3)
3. Instead of completing the Figure Eight, leave baton at left side, turn tip up, palm facing sky. Put other hand (left hand) just over right palm so that hands are touching. Place baton in crook of left thumb. (See Illustration 4).

Illus. 3

4. Right hand is removed.
5. Left thumb takes a firm hold on baton. Turn left hand completely over so that ball is up. (See Illustration 5).
6. Dip across body to right side.

Illus. 4

Illus. 5

Illus. 6

7. Leave baton at right side, turn tip up, left palm is facing sky. Put other hand (right hand) just over left palm so that hands are touching. Place baton in crook of right thumb.

8. Left hand is removed.

9. Right thumb takes a firm hold on baton. Turn hand completely over so that ball is up.

10. Dip across body to left side.

11. . . . REPEAT . . .

TWIRLING FUNDAMENTALS ~ADVANCED

Front Wheel–Left Hand

1. Hold baton in left hand, thumb to ball with hand directly above right foot, elbow straight.

Illus. 1

2. Do one backward wrist twirl (ball coming towards waist), Illustration 1).

3. Stop.

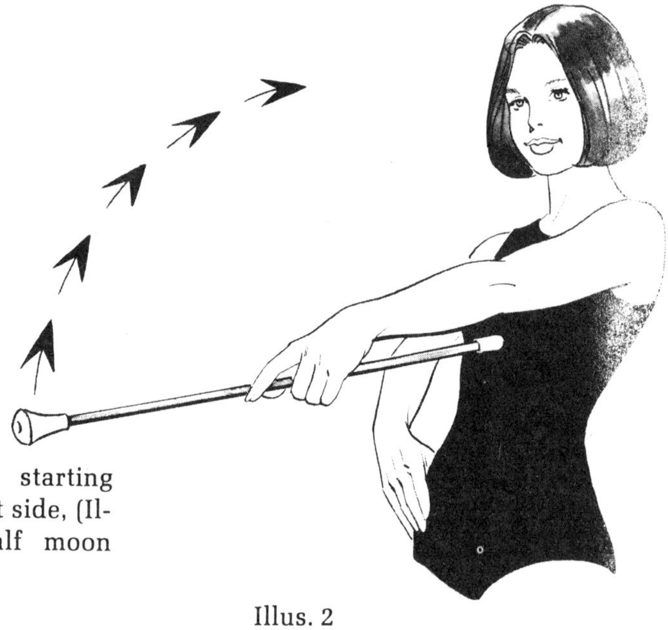

4. Leading with ball and starting from waist levei on right side, (Illustration 2), draw half moon over to left.

Illus. 2

Illus. 3

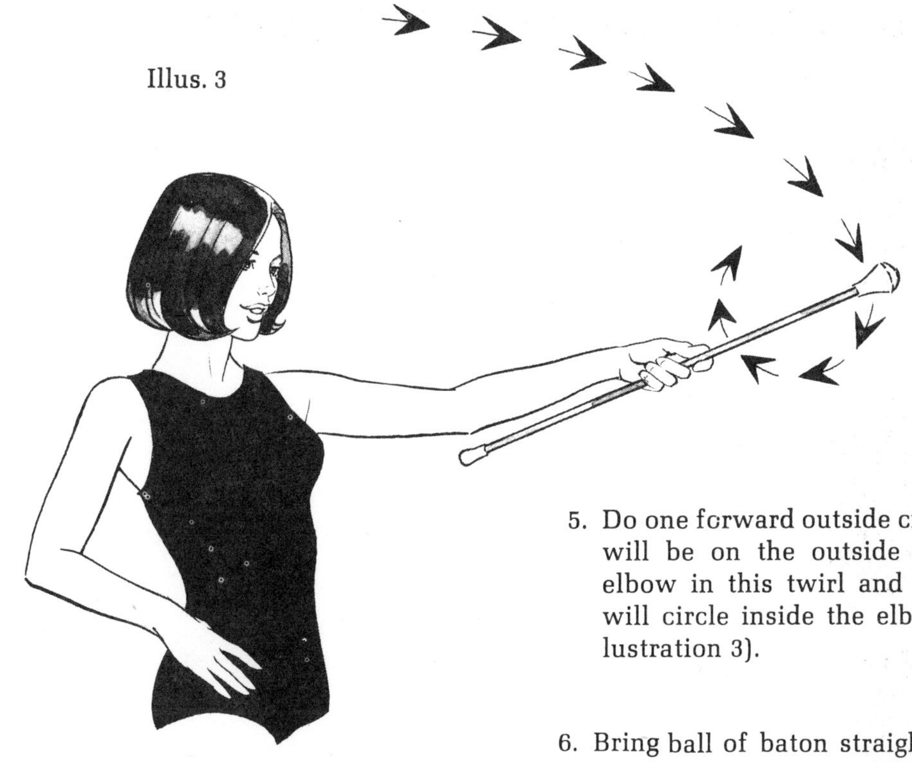

5. Do one forward outside circle (ball will be on the outside of your elbow in this twirl and the tip will circle inside the elbow). (Illustration 3).

6. Bring ball of baton straight down to starting position, (Illustration 4).

Illus 4.

Cartwheel - Catch Behind Back

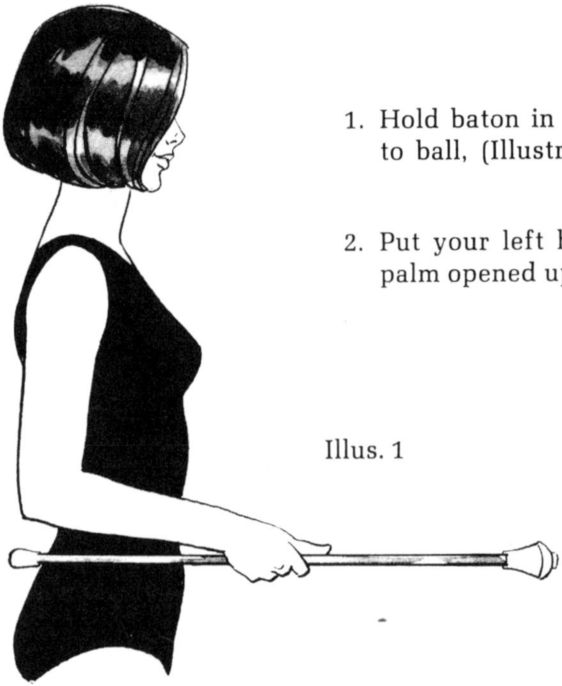

1. Hold baton in right hand, thumb to ball, (Illustration 1).

2. Put your left hand behind back, palm opened upward.

Illus. 1

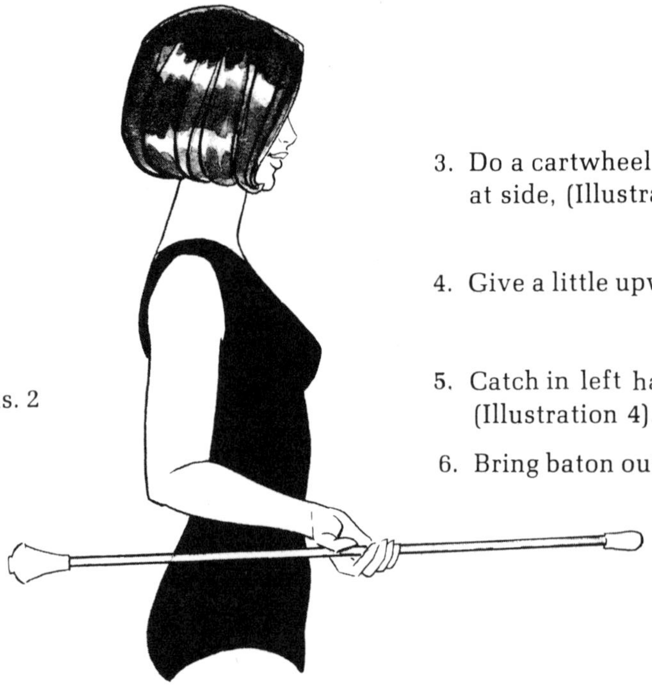

3. Do a cartwheel in your right hand at side, (Illustrations 2 and 3).

4. Give a little upward push.

5. Catch in left hand behind back. (Illustration 4).

6. Bring baton out on left side.

Illus. 2

Illus. 3

7. Put right hand behind back, palm opened upward.

8. Do a cartwheel in your left hand.

9. Give a little upward push.

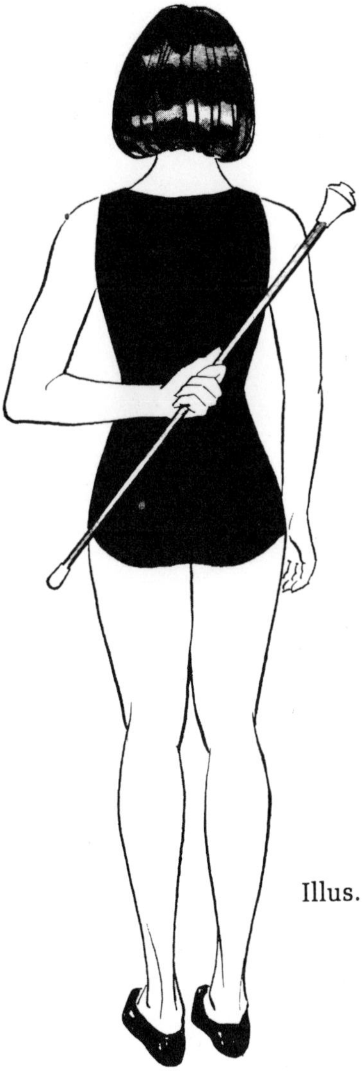

Illus. 4

10. Catch in right hand behind back.

11. Bring to right side to begin twirl again . . .

Cartwheels – Under Legs

1. Hold baton thumb to ball in right hand.

2. Raise right leg and point toe downward.

3. Put left hand under right leg, from inside to outside, (See Illustration 1).

Illus. 1

4. Do cartwheel in right hand, take in left hand. Come out from under leg to left side, (See Illustration 2).

Illus. 2

5. Put right hand under left leg. Do a cartwheel in left hand, (See Illustration 3).

6. Take baton in right hand, come out from under leg to right side, and repeat twirl . . . (Illus. 4)

Illus. 3

Illus. 4

FINGER TWIRLS

Four Finger Twirl

1. Hold baton, ball to the left, between the first and second fingers, (Illustration 1).

2. Turn baton to the second finger, (Illustration 2).

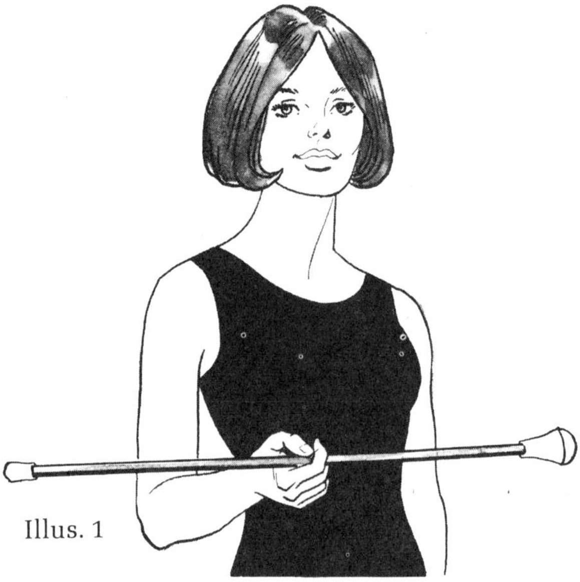

Illus. 1

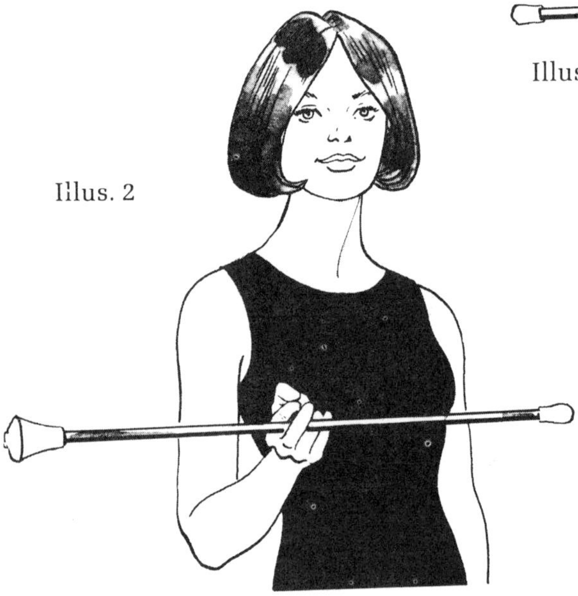

Illus. 2

3. The baton rolls into the third finger, (Illustration 3).

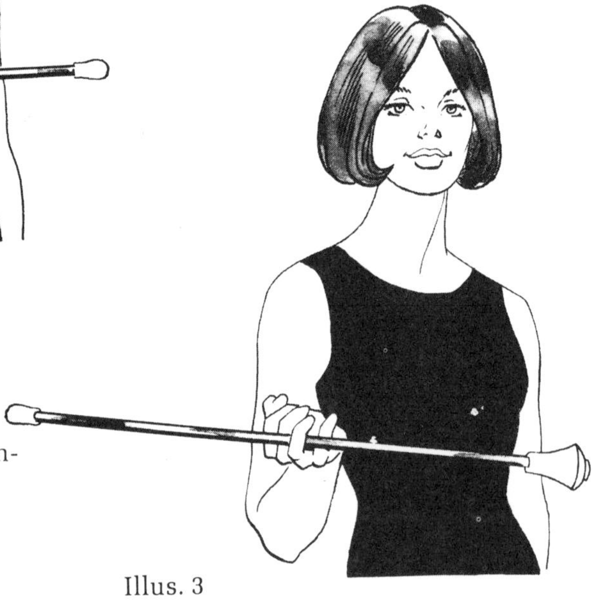

Illus. 3

4. The baton rolls into the little finger, (Illustration 4).

5. Baton rolls out of little finger across back of fingers near knuckles into palm, (Illustration 5).

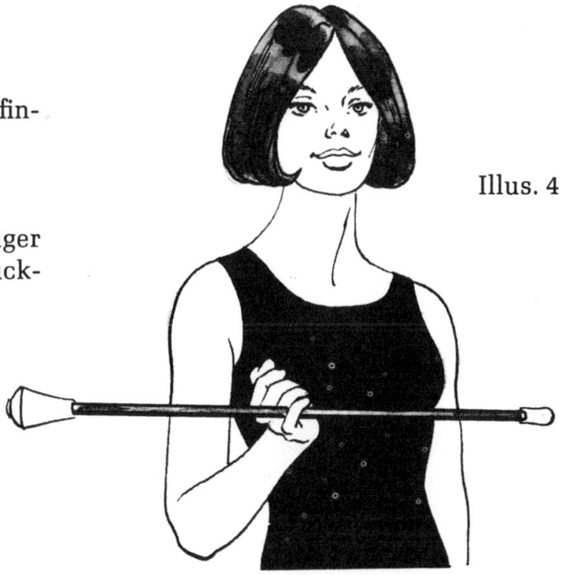

Illus. 4

Illus. 5

6. Your baton is now in a position to begin twirl again, (Illustration 6).

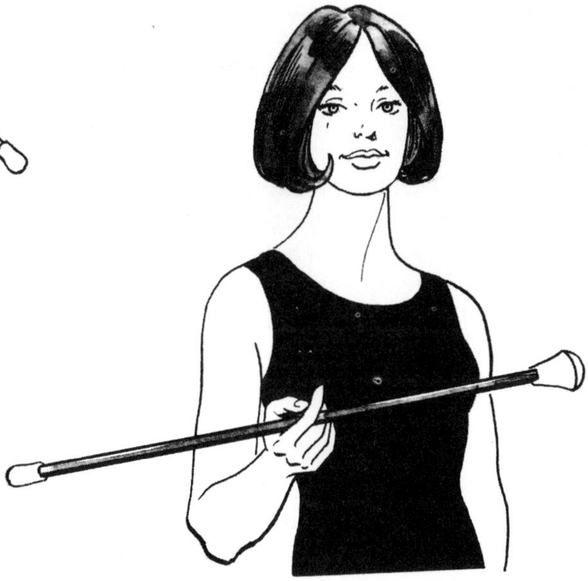

Illus. 6

Figure 8 Finger Twirl

1. Hold baton thumb to ball.

2. Do one complete Figure Eight and one-half of another, (Illustration 1).

Illus. 1

Illus. 2

3. When the ball of the baton comes up on top, it goes through the first two fingers and stops between the middle finger and the ring finger, (Illustration 2).

Illus. 3

4. Dip back down to Figure 8 motion (which is bring the ball towards your body), (Illustration 3).

5. Come back through middle (Illustration 4) to the first (index) finger (Illustration 5).

6. Dip back and begin again, (Illustration 6).

Illus. 4

Illus. 5

Important: Keep little finger and ring finger together. The baton never goes through these fingers in this twirl. I would suggest while practicing this twirl that you tape your ring finger to your little finger until you learn the twirl well.

Illus. 6

Horizontal Split Finger Twirl

1. Hold baton, ball to the left, between your first and second finger, (Illustration 1).

2. Turn baton in a horizontal position to second finger, (Illustration 2).

3. Turn baton in a horizontal position to third finger, (Illustration 3).

Illus. 1

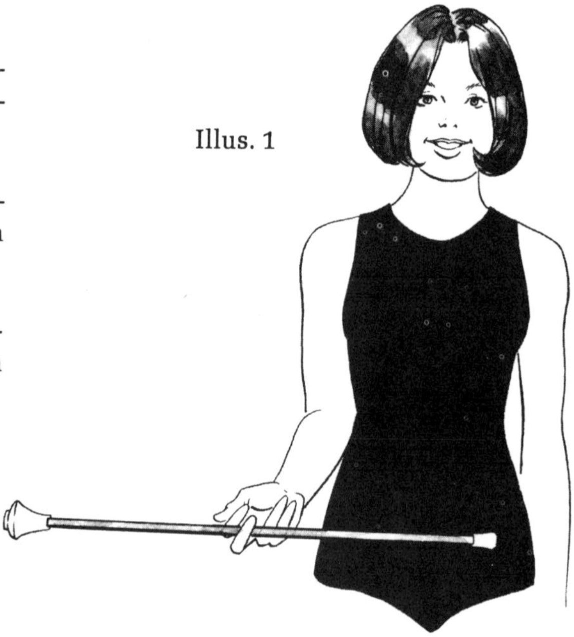

Illus. 2

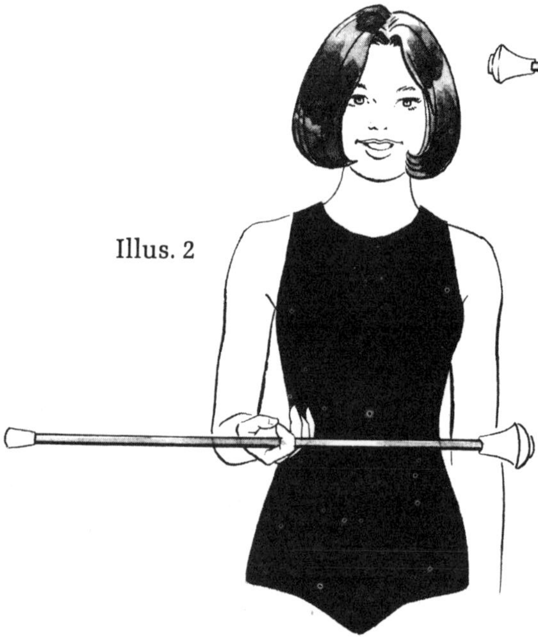

(It would be helpful to tape your fourth finger to your third finger. You never go past your third finger.)

Illus. 3

4. In a horizontal twirl bring ball of baton under arm, (See also Illustration 3).

5. Keep baton twirling and raise hand to Illustration 4.

6. Turn baton to middle finger, (Illustration 5).

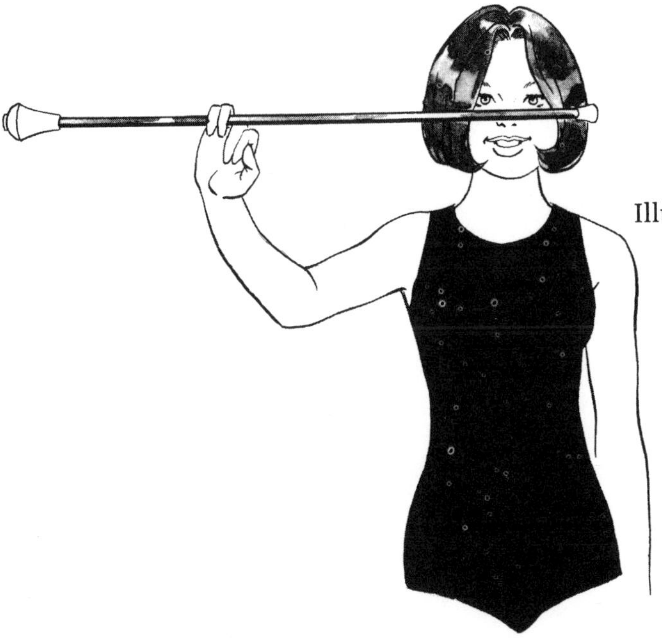

Illus. 4

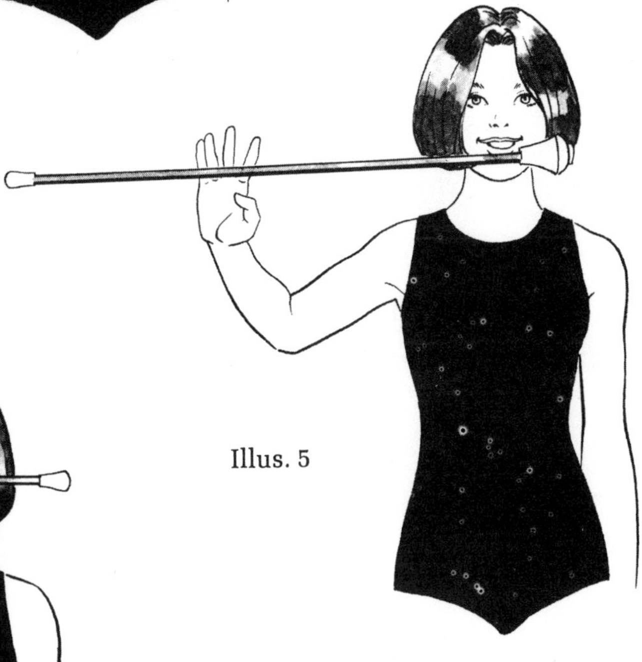

Illus. 5

Illus. 6

7. Turn baton to index finger, (Illustration 6).

8. To begin twirl again, lower baton while still in first finger, (See Illustration 1).

TRICKS AND NOVELTY

Lariat Rope

1. Hold ball of baton loosely, draw horizontal circle going from left to right, tip towards ground, (Illustration 1).

2. Then circle over head one time from left shoulder to right shoulder making the twirl flat as a plate. (Illustration 2).

3. When you get to right shoulder bring baton in front of you. (Illustration 3).

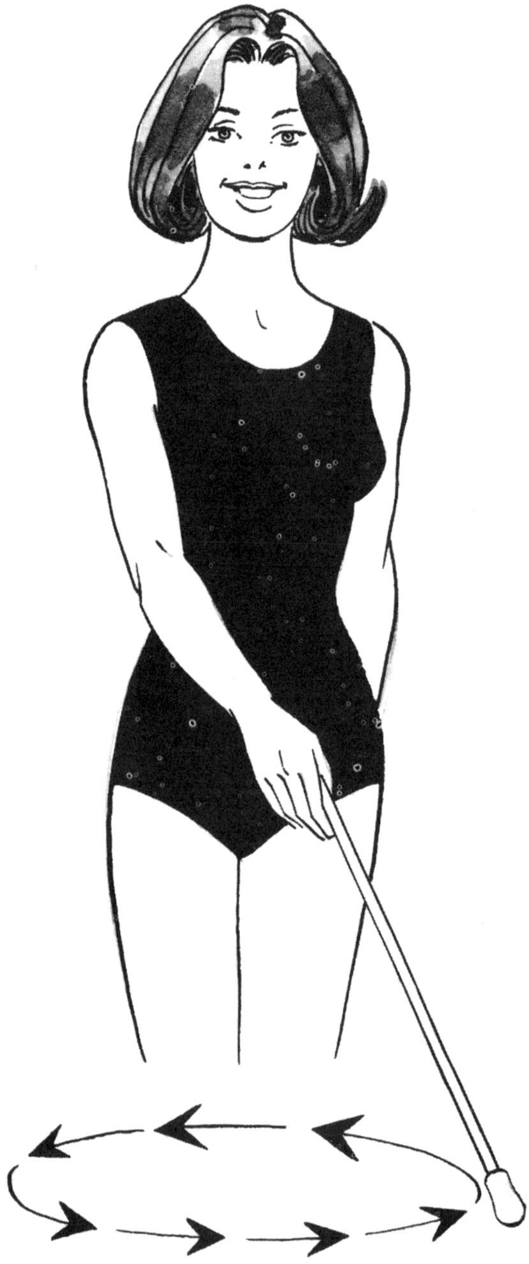

Illus. 1

Illus. 2

Illus. 3

(continued next page)

Lariat Rope

(continued)

4. Lift leg straight out front, point toe and move the baton under the left raised leg (Illustration 4). Quickly put that left leg down and lift the right leg straight out front pointing toe and continue moving the baton under the right leg (Illustration 5).

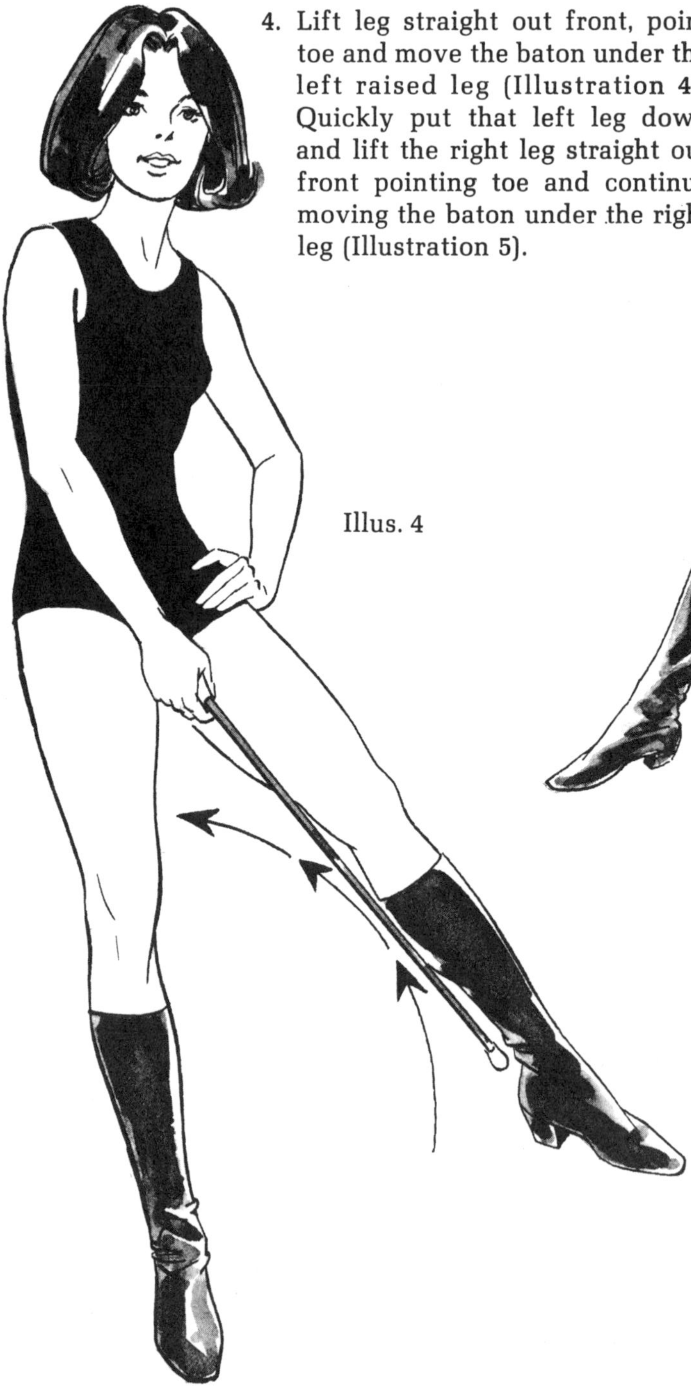

Illus. 4

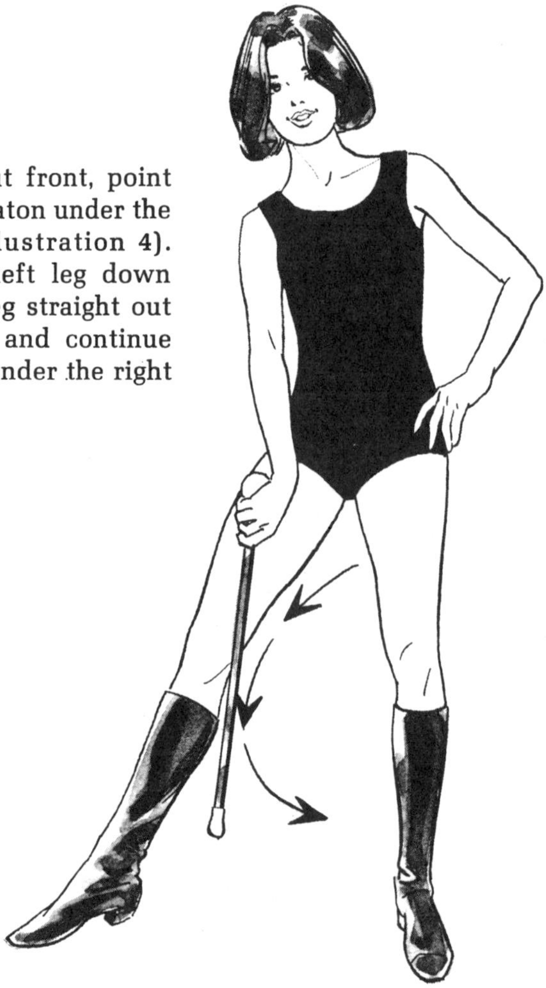

Illus. 5

Lariat Rope Around Ankle

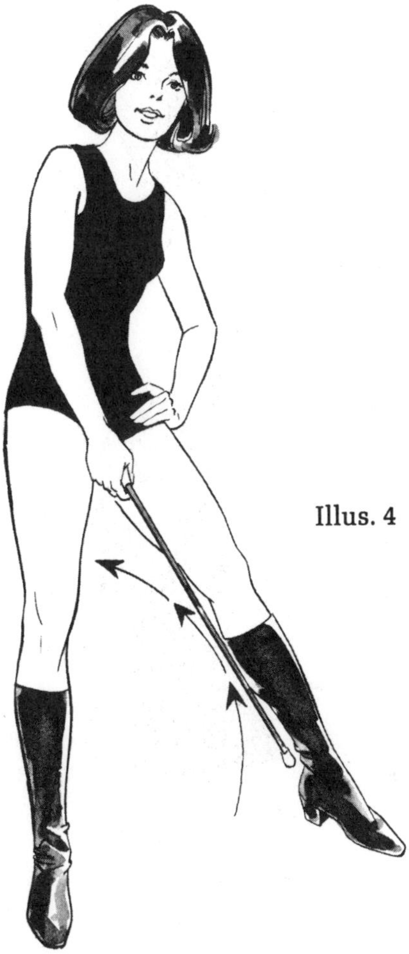

Illus. 4

Do Rope Twirl 1, 2, and 3.

4. Lift left leg straight out, (Illustration 4). Point toe and move baton under the left raised leg.

5. Quickly put that left leg down and lift the right knee waist high with toe pointed down.

Illus. 5

6. Let baton roll in a horizontal position across front of right ankle, (See Illustration 5).

7. Catch in left hand (See same Illustration).

Body Roll

1. Hold baton in **left** hand at the tip. Take a wide complete swing around body (left to right). (Illustration 1).

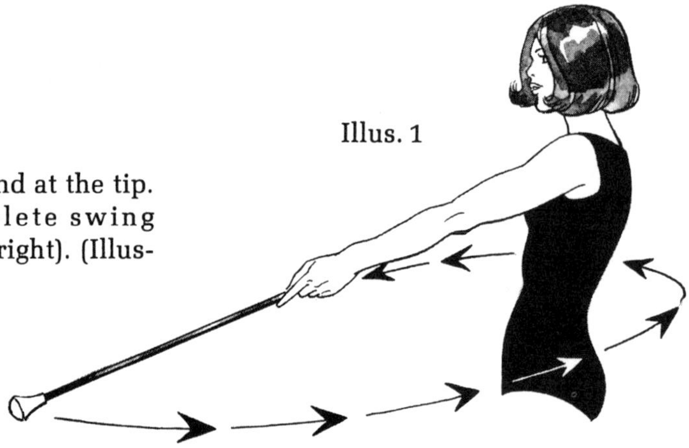

Illus. 1

2. As the baton reaches the right side, let the shaft hit the body about two-thirds down from the ball. (Illustration 2).

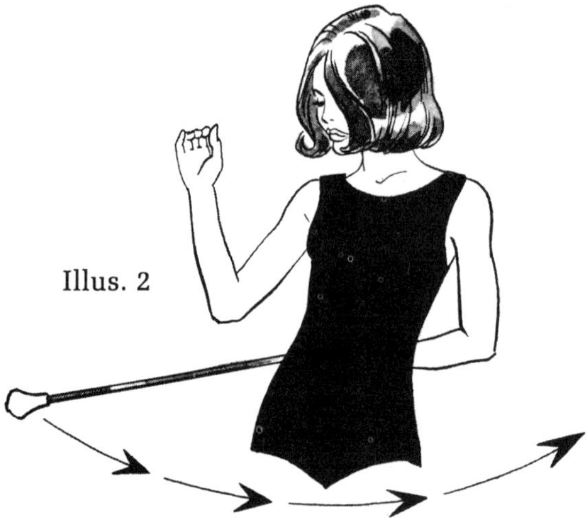

Illus. 2

3. The catch will be made with the **right** hand in back of the body. (Illustration 3).

Illus. 3

Helpful Hints: The catch with the right hand in back of the body will be easier if you raise your left hand straight up and out of your way as you are catching it. If you prefer you can just make sure the right hand is on the outside of the left hand for the catch.

Palm Spin

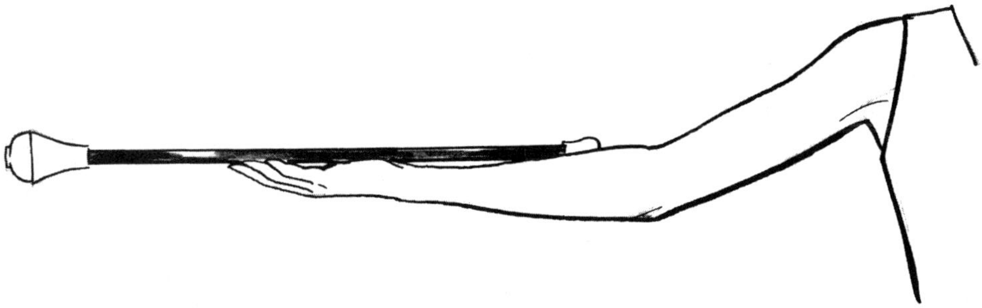

1. Do the Horizontal Twirl (Ball on Top, Tip on Bottom)

2. Open hand flat—fingers together.

3. Let baton spin on palm slowly.

4. Take back into Horizontal Twirl.

Note: Practice this twirl feet together, back straight, head high. When one hand is not in use, it is placed on waist or hip, fingers together.

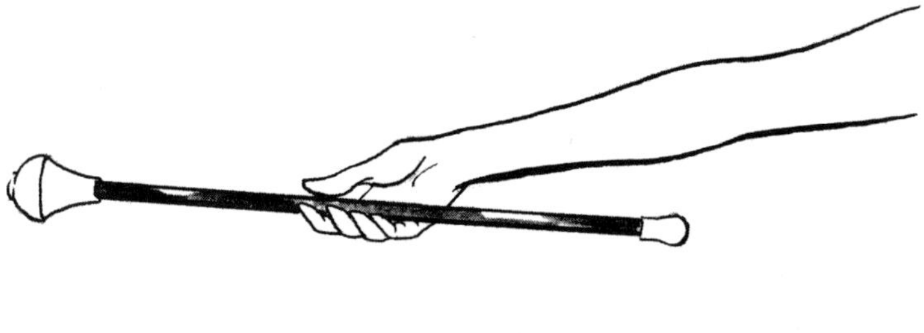

Palm Spin Over Head

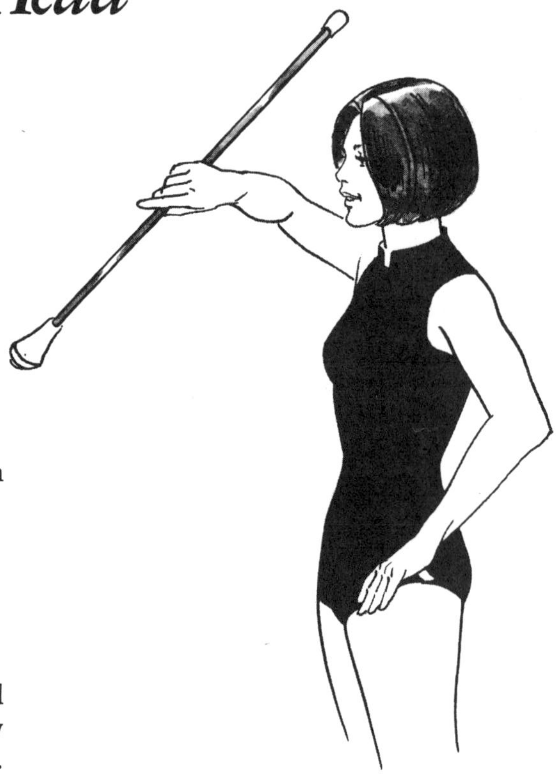

1. Do several horizontal twirls in your right hand.
2. Stop.
3. With wrist leading towards head bring hand and baton directly over head knuckles touching hair.
4. Open palm very flat and let baton spin around on flattened hand.
5. Take back into horizontal twirl and lower to extreme right.
6. Try it again . . .

Helpful Hints: Remember to keep the palm close to the top of the head so if it falls, it will fall away from your head and your body.

Fingertip Twirl

1. Do Horizontal Twirl, stop, make table of fingers.

2. Move the baton around with your thumb as the baton stays on top of your four fingers.

3. The idea of the twirl is to make the motion of the baton flat as a plate, being careful to keep the plate horizontal so that the food doesn't fall from it.

4. Take baton back into hand and do Horizontal Twirl to end it.

Note: Practice this twirl feet together, back straight, head high. When one hand is not in use, it is placed on waist or hip, fingers together.

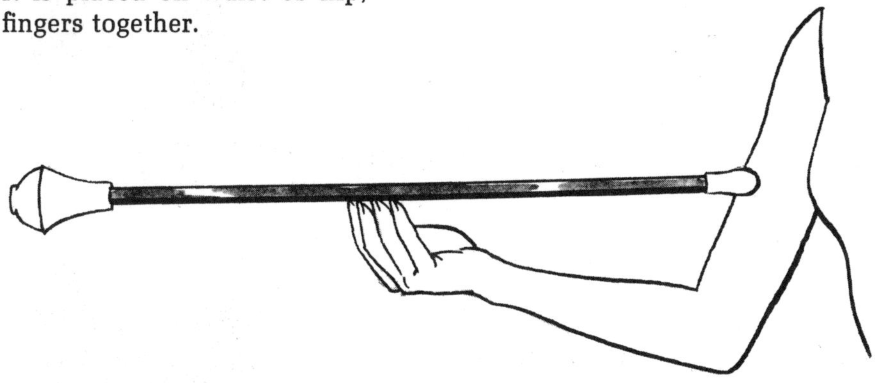

Corkscrew (Grapevine)

1. Hold baton in right hand by the ball. Circle over head and bring baton around back of neck. Grasp with left hand, (Illustration 1).

Illus. 1

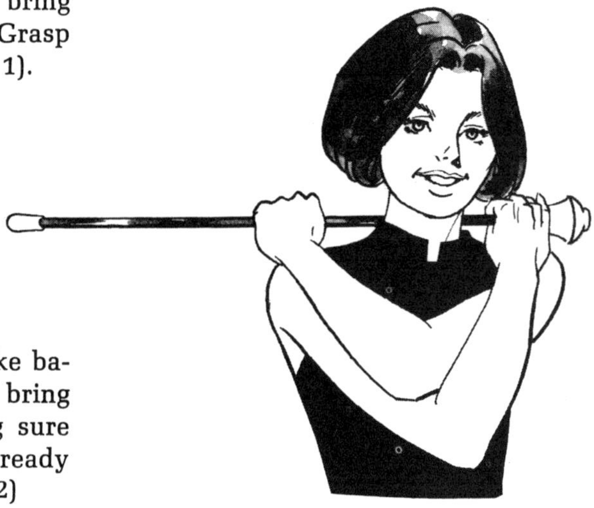

2. Push hand down to tip. Take baton by tip in left hand and bring baton around back making sure right arm **is on the outside,** ready for the catch. (Illustration 2)

3. Roll across waist, catch in right hand which is at left side, (Illustration 3).

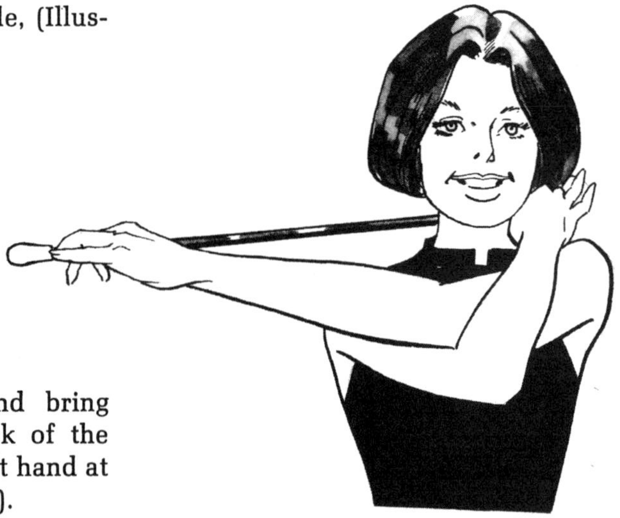

4. Take in right hand and bring across front to the back of the knees and grasp with left hand at right side, (Illustration 4).

Illus. 2

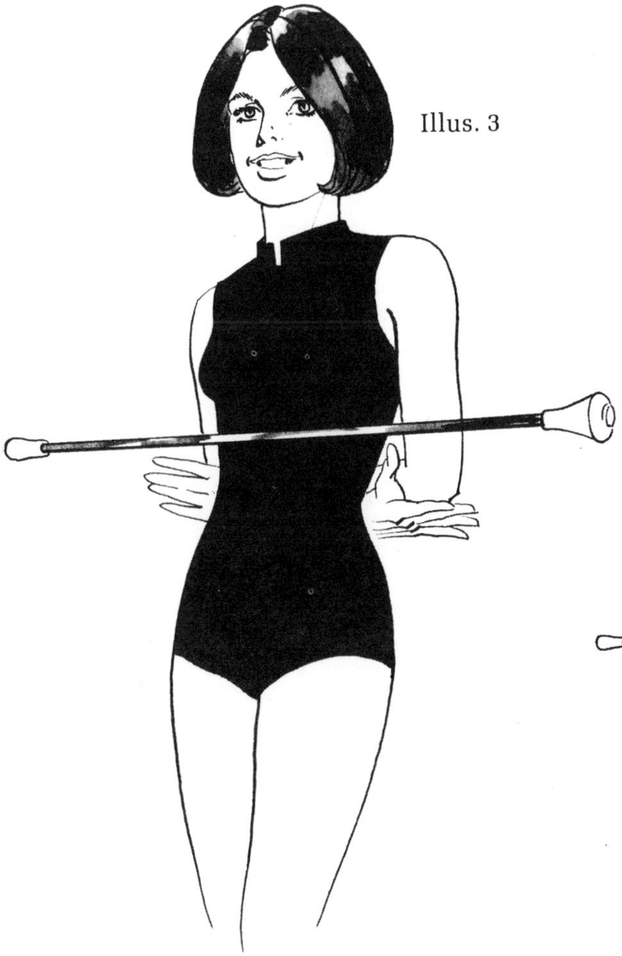

Illus. 3

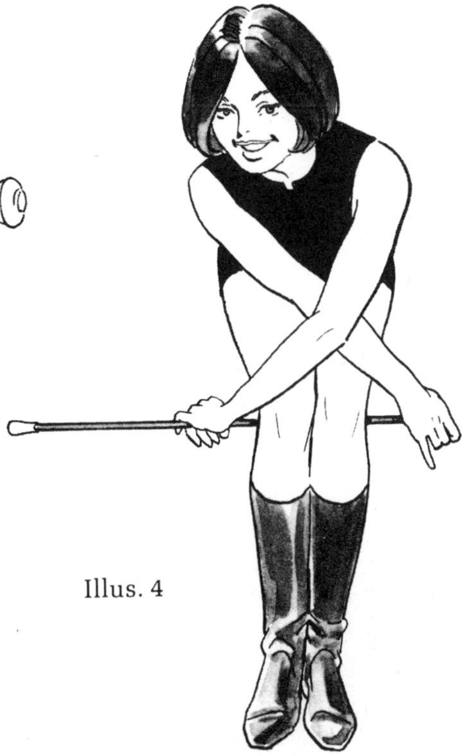

Illus. 4

Slide to tip and bring baton across front to back of ankle.

5. Roll across front of ankles and catch in right hand, (Illustration 5).

Illus. 5

Leg Roll 1

1. Hold tip of baton in right hand.

2. Bring right leg up level with toe pointed downward.

3. Bring baton under right leg (See Illustration 1).

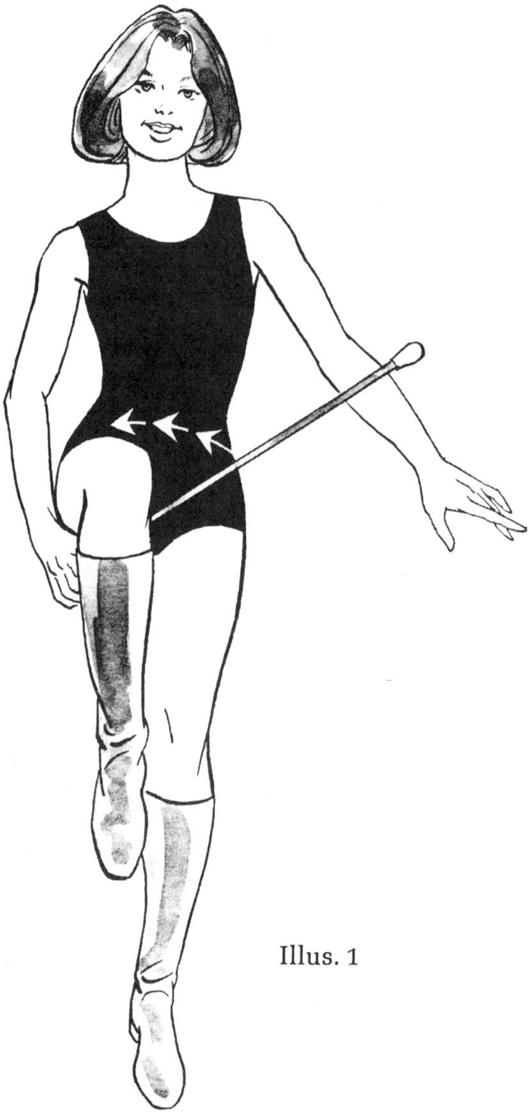

Illus. 1

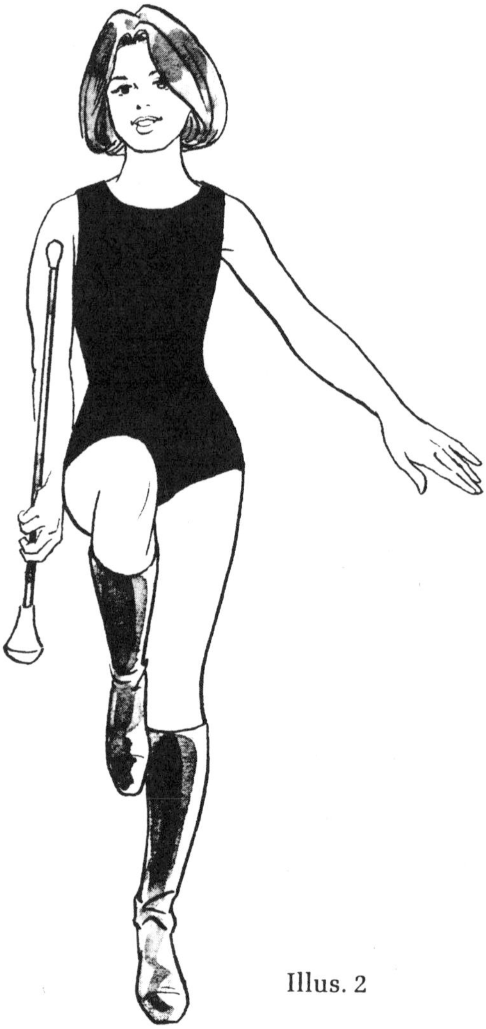

Illus. 2

4. As soon as you release baton to roll across top of right leg, press knuckles of right hand into outside of right leg (See Illustration 2). Open hand to receive baton.

Leg Roll 2

Illus. 1

1. Hold baton in right hand by the ball or large end.

2. Make one large circle in front. (See Illustration 1).

3. Bring left leg up level with toe pointed down.

4. Bring baton under left leg (See Illustration 2).

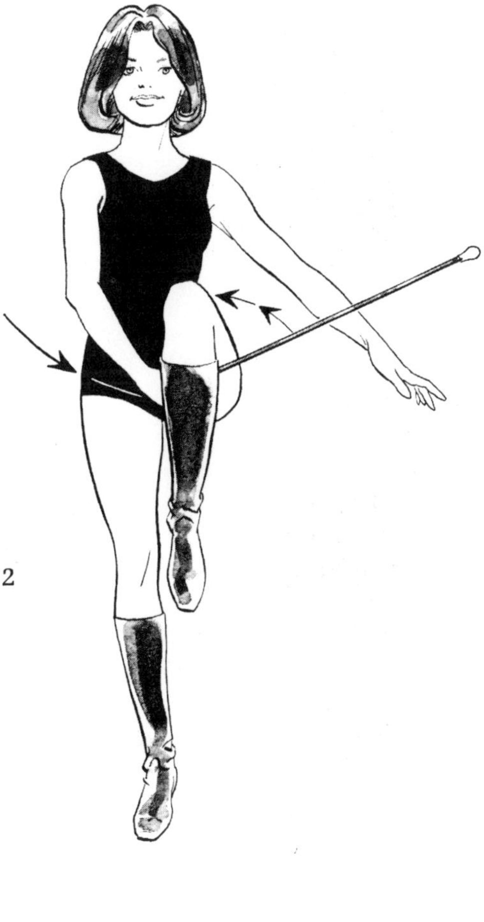

Illus. 2

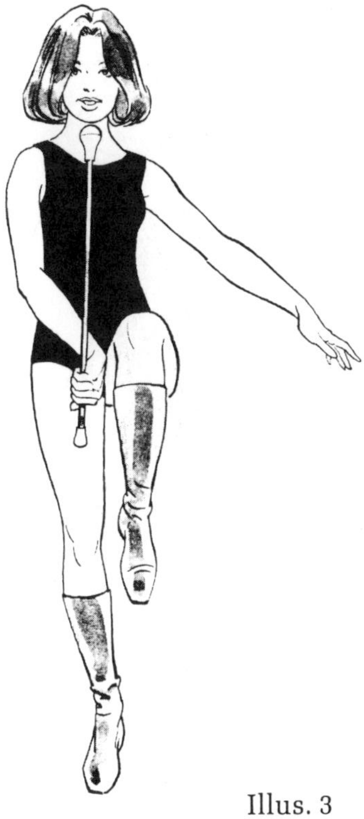

Illus. 3

5. As soon as you release baton to roll across top of left leg, press knuckles of right hand into inside of left leg (See Illustration 3). Open hand to receive baton.

Leg Roll 3

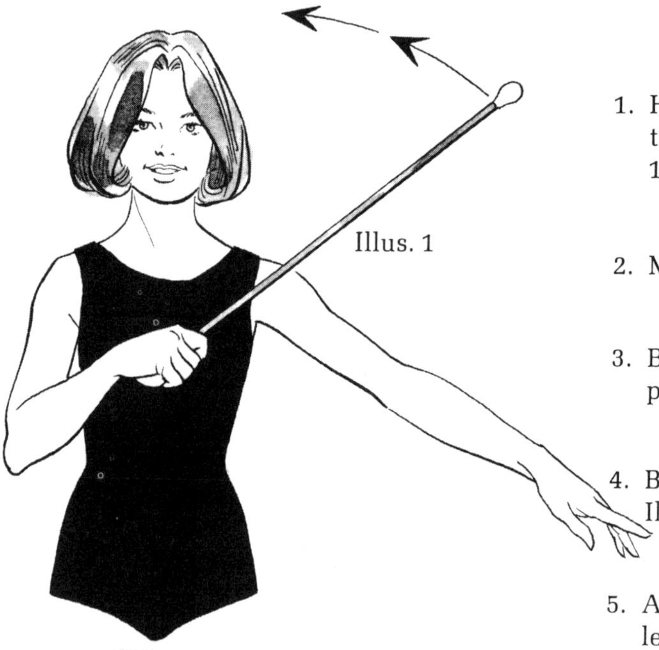

Illus. 1

1. Hold baton in right hand by the tip or small end (See Illustration 1).

2. Make one large circle in front.

3. Bring left leg up level with toe pointed down.

4. Bring baton under left leg (See Illustration 2).

5. As baton is rolling across top of left leg (from your left to your right) left hand reaches under left leg to catch baton. (See Illustration 3)

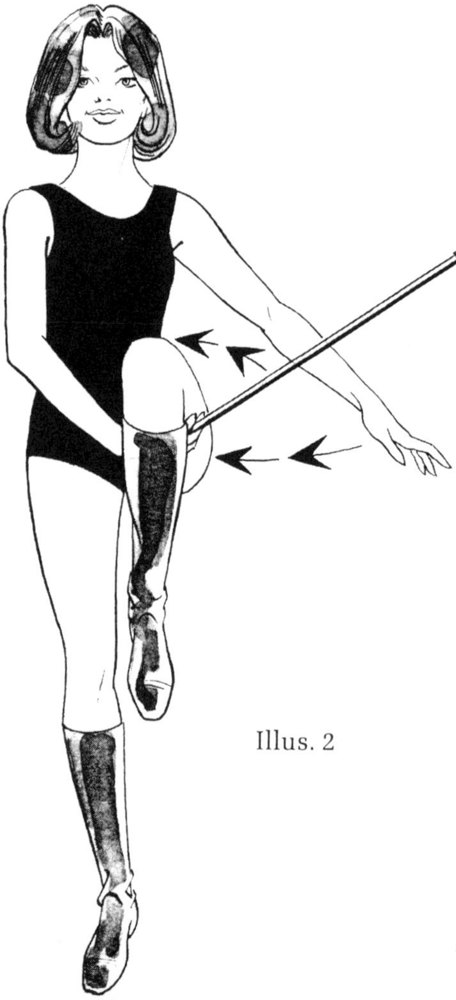

Illus. 2

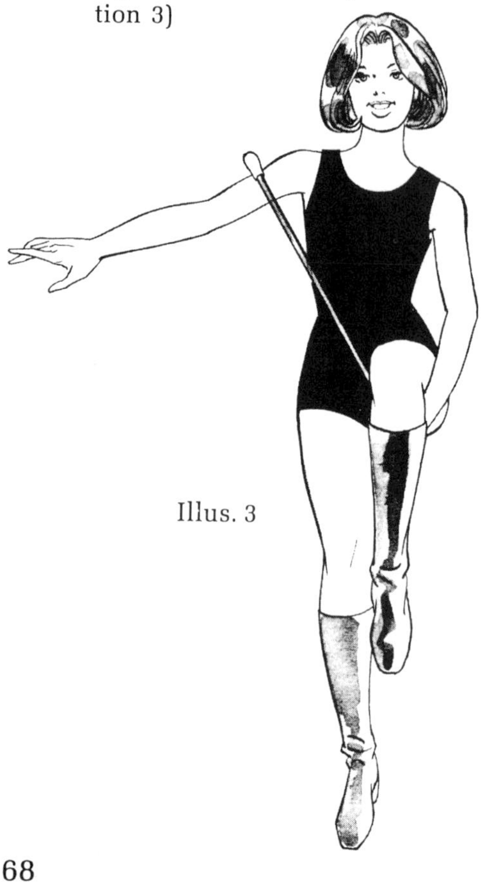

Illus. 3

Leg Roll 3 with Ankle Roll

1. Do Leg Roll #3 Twirl.

2. Hold baton by ball, thumb pointing to the tip.

3. Bring foot and leg to your left until foot is in back and level with knee.

4. Roll baton over left ankle and catch with left hand on top of back of ankle.

Elbow Roll

1. Hold baton in right hand three-fourths of the way down the shaft, thumb pointing to the ball. Place your left fist in the middle of your chest, elbow bent and arm in a horizontal position level to shoulder. (Illustration 1)

Illus. 1

Illus. 2

2. Bring baton under bent elbow which is in horizontal position and let baton roll across top of left elbow. (Give your elbow a little upward push as baton is rolling across it.) (Illustrations 2 and 2a)

3. Catch the baton on the right side of your body in a vertical position (straight up & down) with your thumb pointing to the ball.

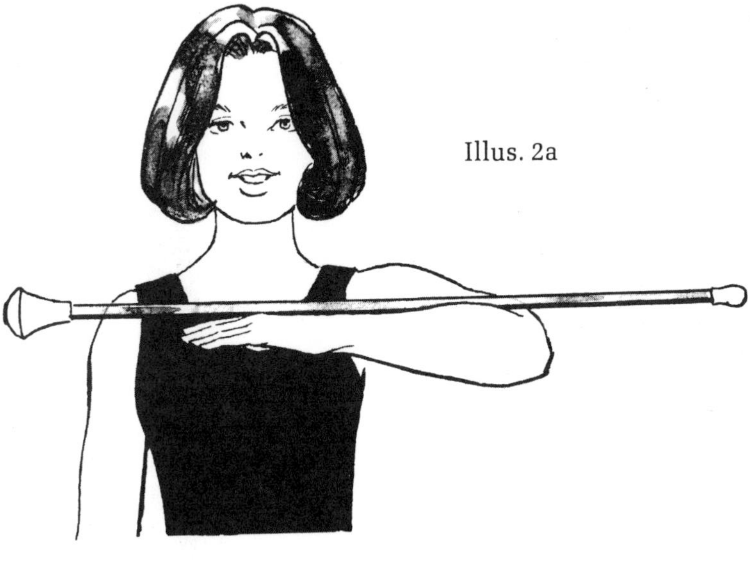

Illus. 2a

Double Elbow Roll

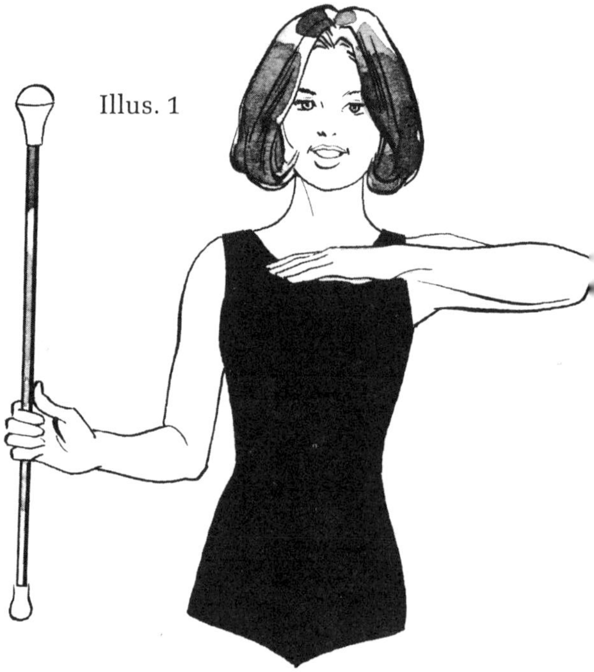

Illus. 1

1. Hold baton in right hand three-fourths of the way down shaft, thumb pointing to the ball. Place your left fist in the middle of your chest, elbow bent and arm in a horizontal position level to shoulder. (Illustration 1)

Illus. 2

2. Bring baton under bent elbow which is in horizontal position and let baton roll across top of elbow. (Give your elbow a little upward push as baton is rolling across it.) (Illustrations 2 and 2a)

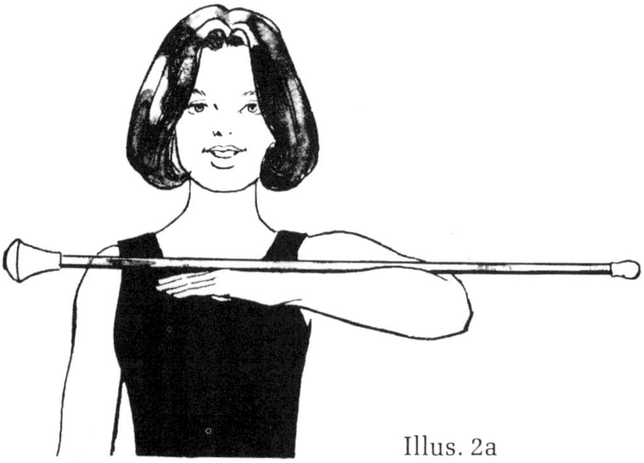

Illus. 2a

3. As soon as you release baton to roll over left elbow immediately bring right elbow up over right end of baton. Push down with right elbow. Baton rolls over right elbow. (Illustrations 3 and 3a)

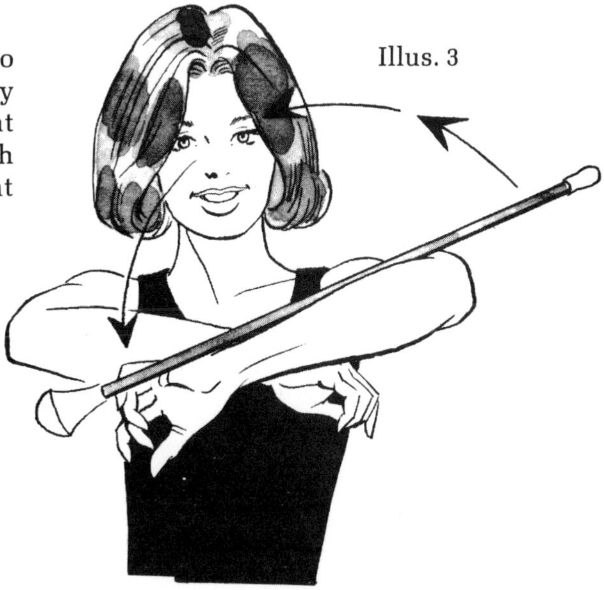

Illus. 3

Illus. 3a

Illus. 4

4. Quickly reach under right elbow with left hand and catch baton thumb to ball (Illustration 4).

Suspender Wraps

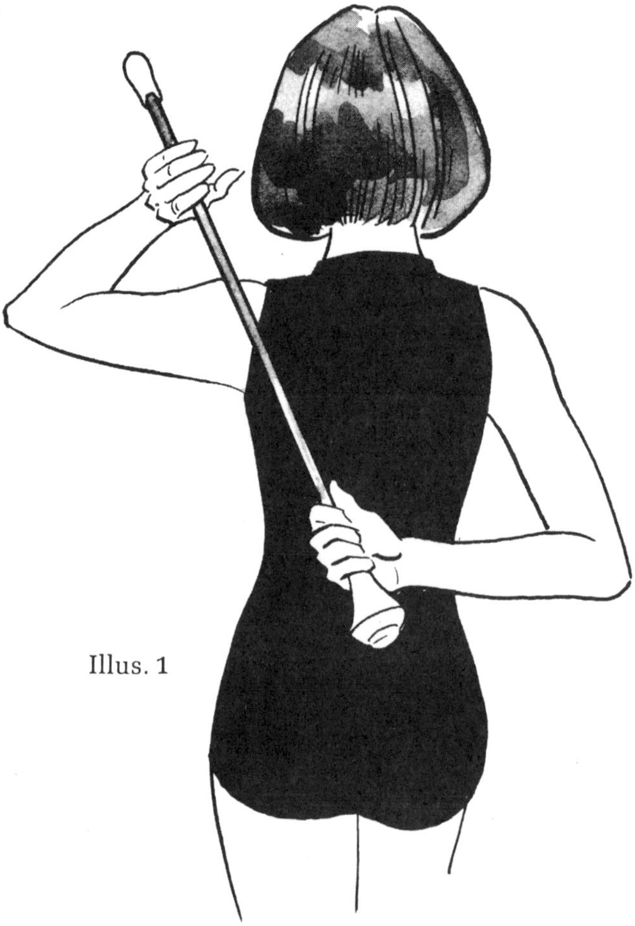

1. Hold baton in right hand by ball.

2. Bring baton behind back to left shoulder. (Illustration 1).

3. With left hand reach up and grasp baton. (Illustration 1).

Illus. 1

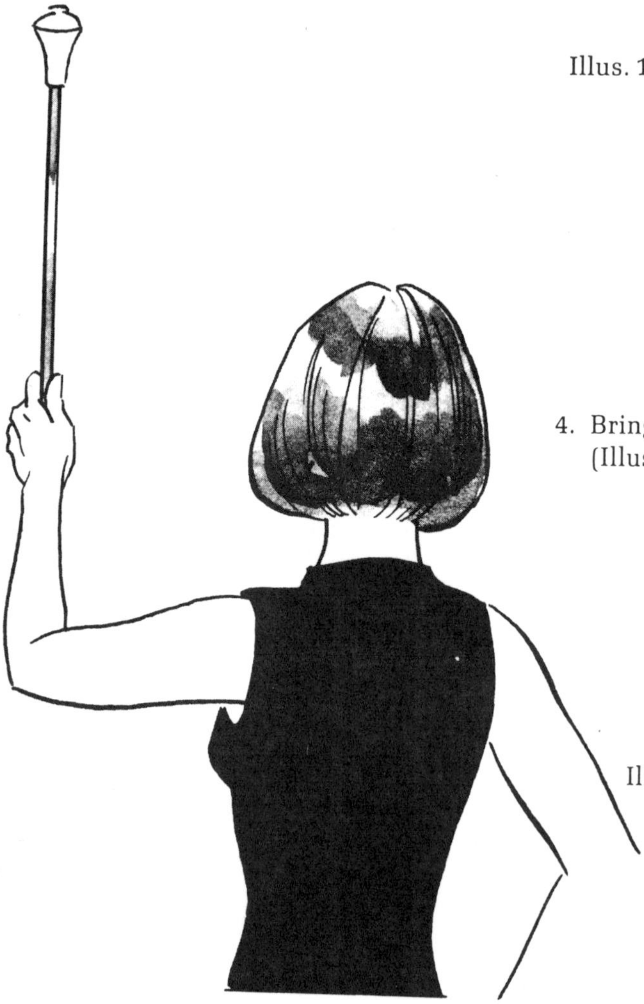

4. Bring baton straight up in air. (Illustration 2).

Illus. 2

Illus. 3

5. Bring baton behind back to right shoulder. (Illustration 3).

6. Reach up with right hand and grasp baton. (Illustration 4).

7. Bring baton straight up in air.

8. Begin twirl again . . .

Illus. 4

Horizontal Leg Bounce

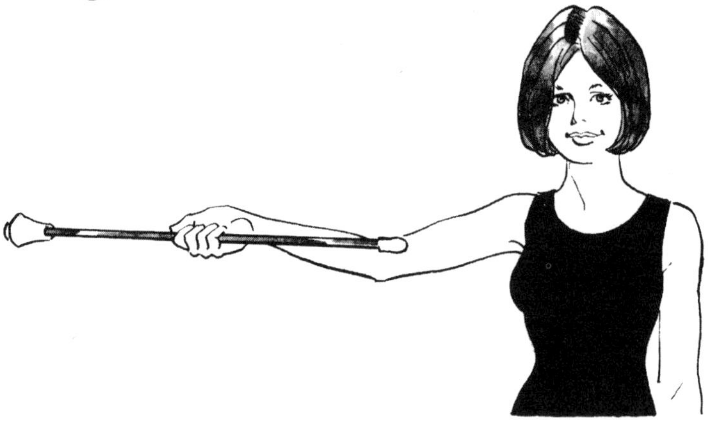

1. Hold the baton in your right hand, thumb to ball.

2. Begin your horizontal twirl. While the baton is twirling, give the baton a little toss upward and to your right and bounce baton off extended outside portion right leg.

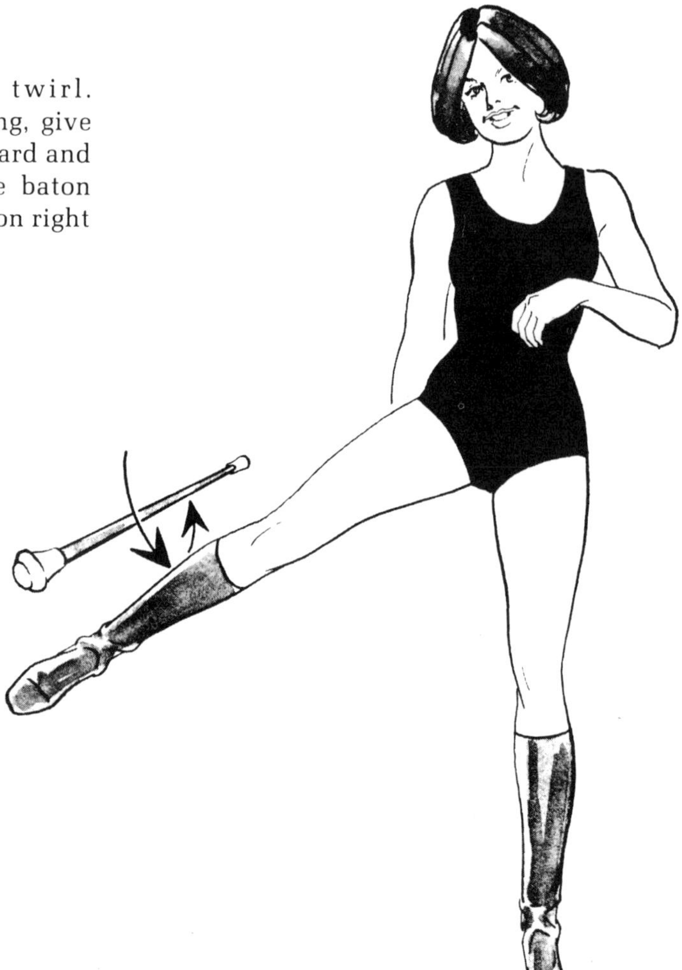

STRIKE ZONE

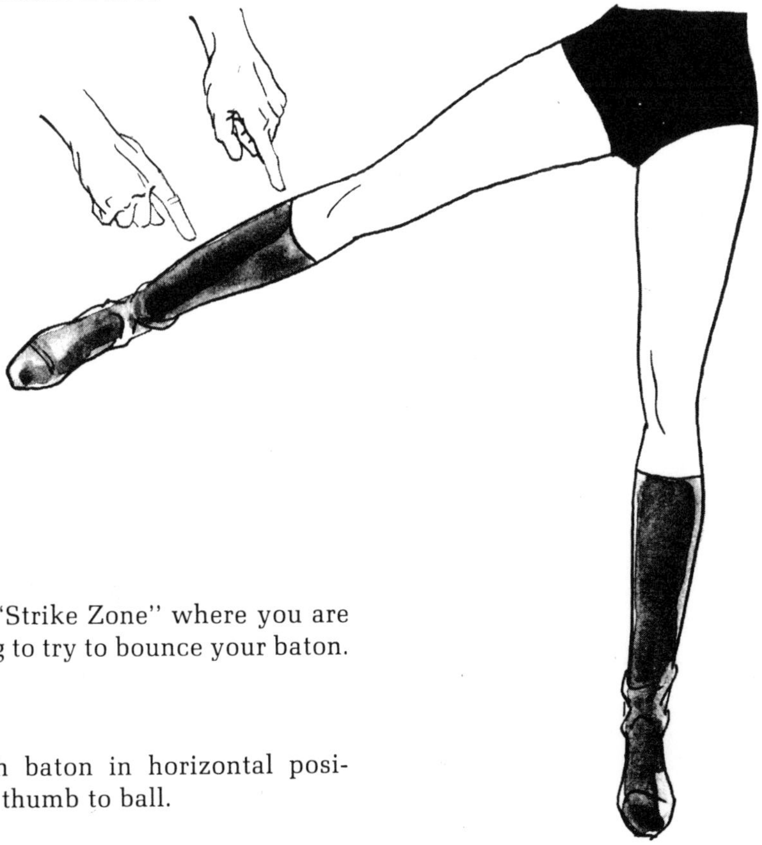

3. See "Strike Zone" where you are going to try to bounce your baton.

4. Catch baton in horizontal position, thumb to ball.

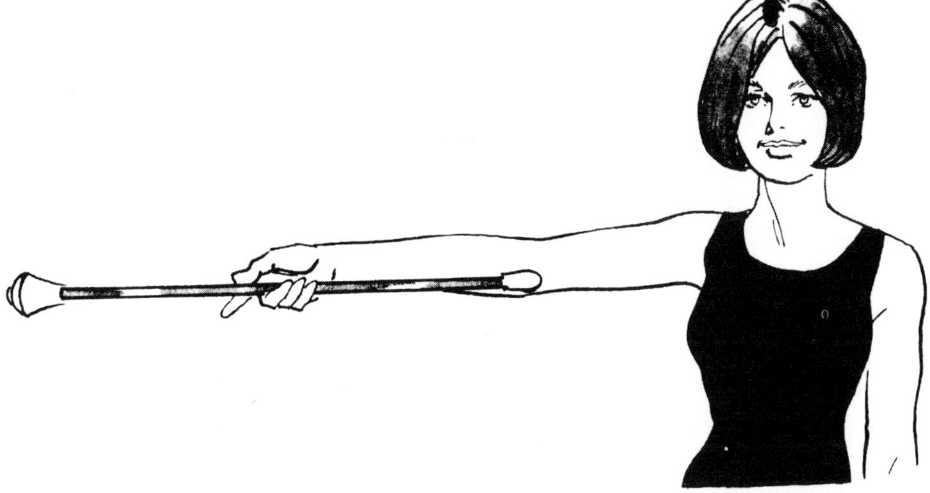

JUMPS AND LEAPS

Straddle Jump 1

1. Standing feet together, do two Front Hand Spins—Stop.

2. Jump with your feet about two feet apart—lock knees, bend forward at waist.

3. Bring ball of baton between legs until tip is past legs (Illustration 3)—turn baton around and bring ball out (Illustration 4).

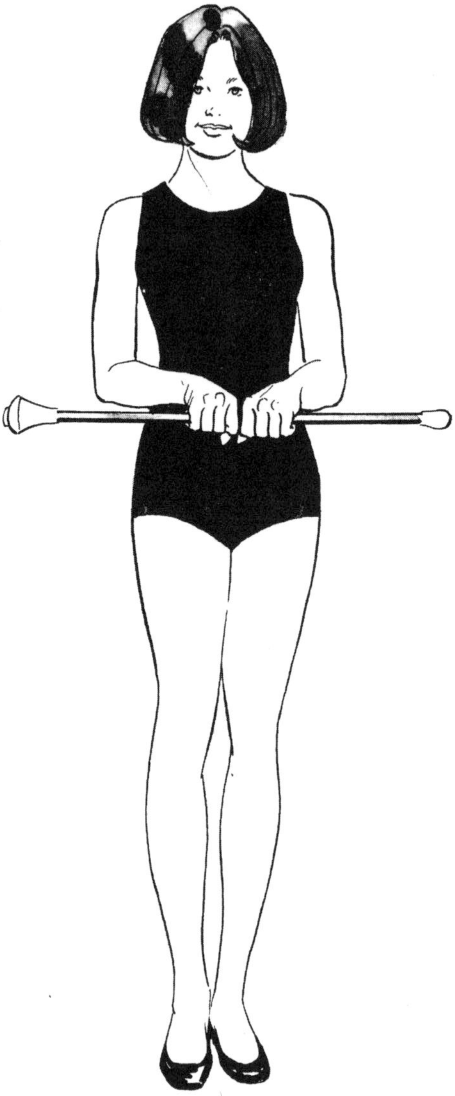

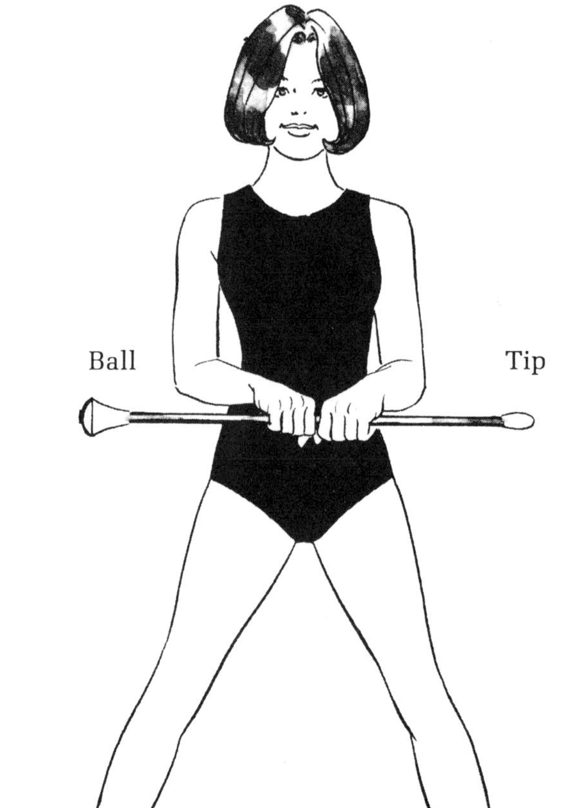

4. As you bring ball out, jump, bring feet together.

5. Finish with two Front Hand Spins.

Illus. 3

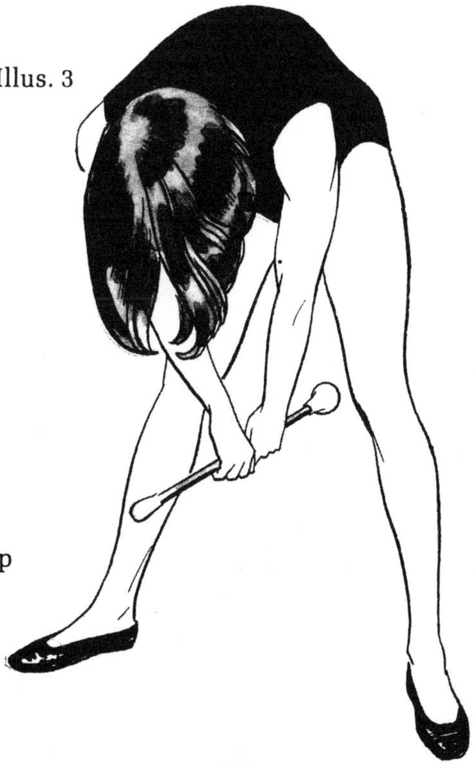

Note: Practice this doing several Front Hand Spins before you jump and make sure you bend from the waist nice and straight and lock your knees and keep your feet pointing straight ahead.

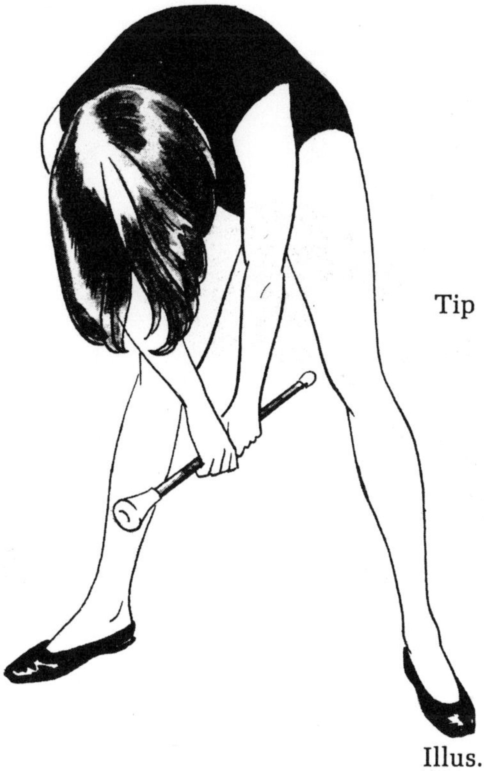

Illus. 4

Straddle Jump 2

1. Hold baton directly over head, ball in right hand, tip in left hand arms straight up in air, elbows locked (Illustration 1)

2. Jump with your feet about two feet apart — lock knees — bend forward at waist. (Illustration 2).

Illus. 1

Illus. 2

Illus. 3

Tip

Ball

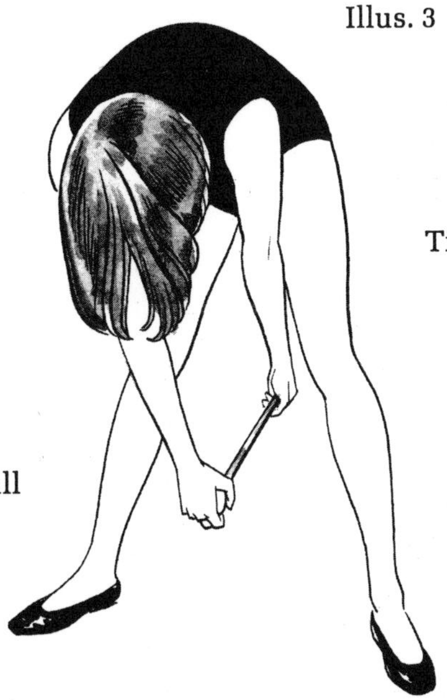

Ball

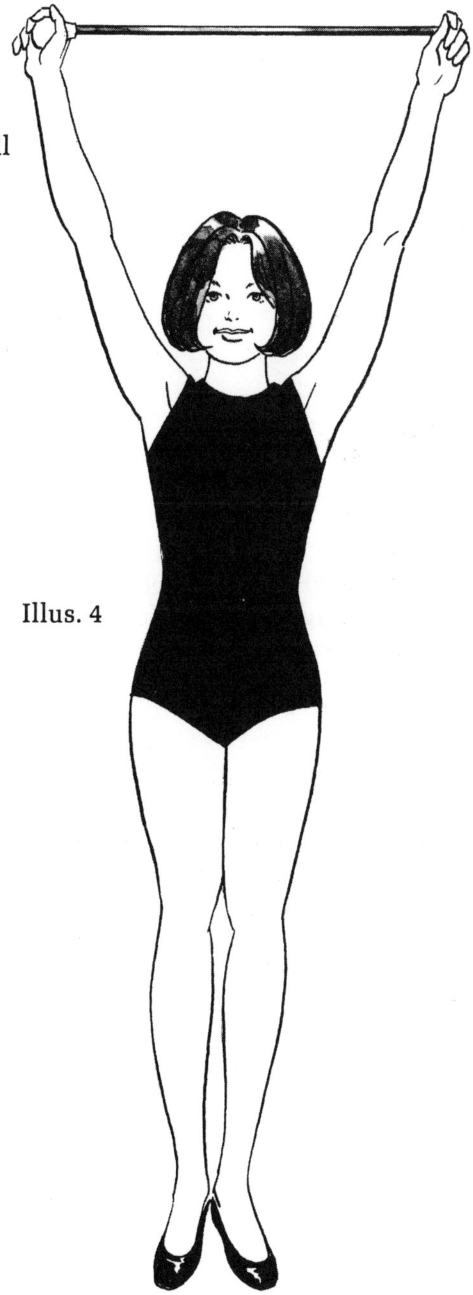

Illus. 4

3. Bring ball of baton between legs until tip is past legs (Illustration 2) then turn baton around and bring ball out (Illustration 3).

4. As you bring ball out, jump, bring feet together. Bring baton over head to starting position to end twirl. (Illustration 4).

Split Jump

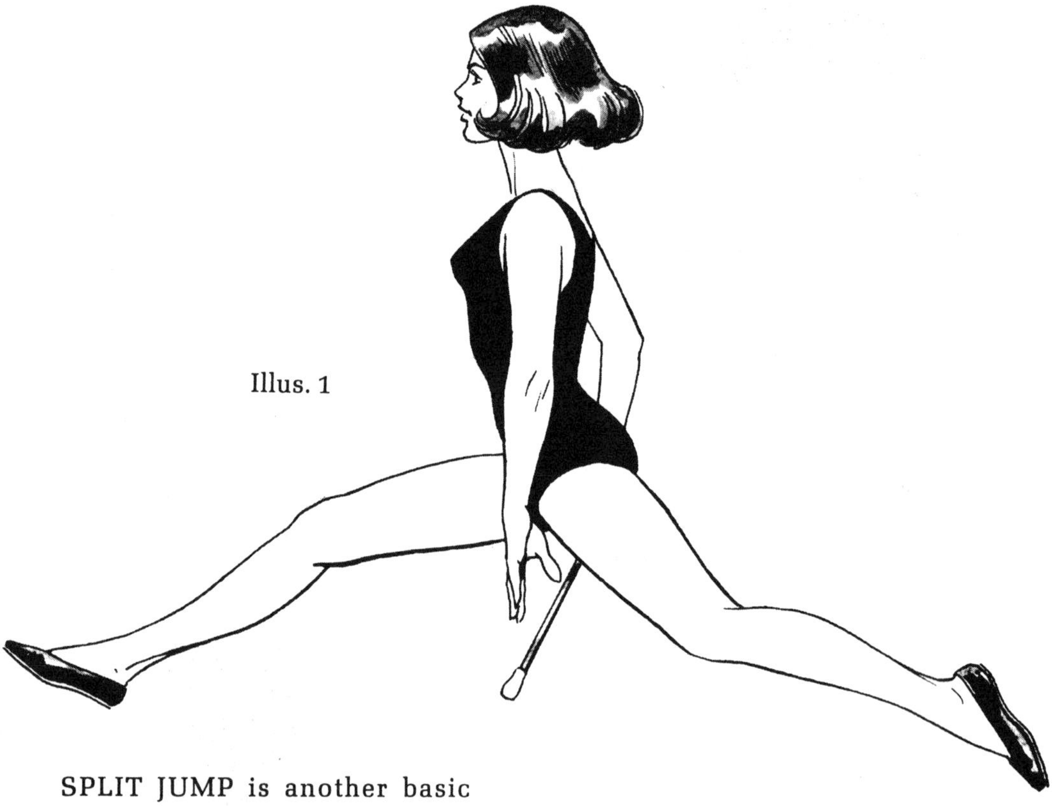

Illus. 1

SPLIT JUMP is another basic jump where your right leg is fairly straight out in front and your left leg is fairly straight out in back.

Helpful Hints: Bend knees slightly just before leaving the ground. Spring from front portion or ball of your foot. Strive to keep both legs as straight as possible. Land on front portion of foot rather than flat footed. Practice is the secret of good jumping.

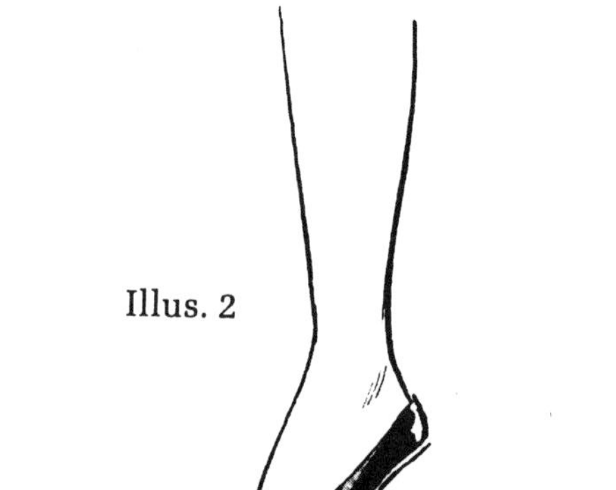

Illus. 2

Spread Eagle Jump

SPREAD EAGLE is the basic jump where you spring up from the front portion or ball of foot and bring legs out as far as possible on each side.

Helpful Hints: Bend knees slightly just before leaving the ground. Practice is the only thing that will help you become a good jumper. You get your spring from the front portion or ball of your foot (See Illustration 2). Land on ball or front portion rather than flat footed.

Illus. 3

AERIALS

High Aerial in Front By Tip

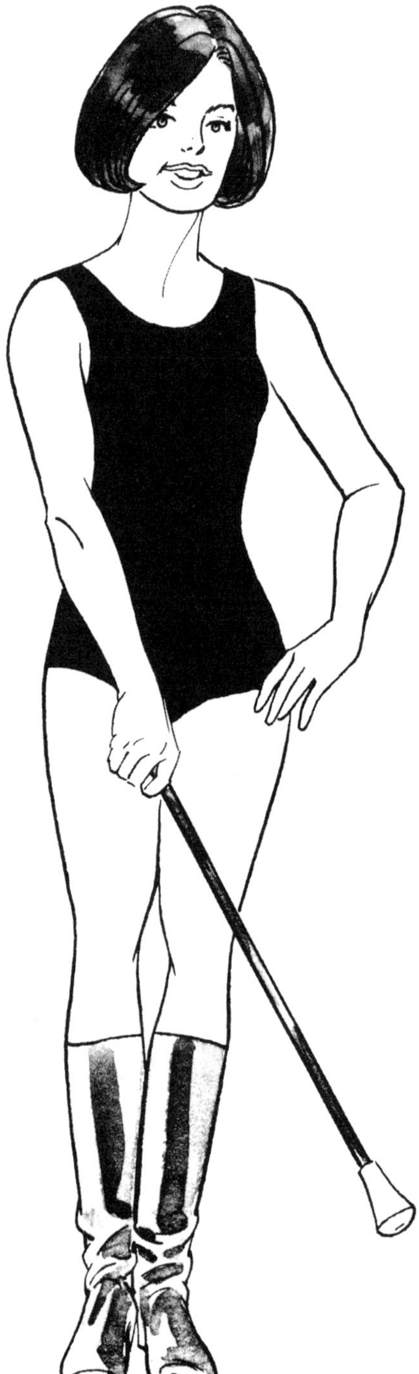

1. Hold baton by tip in right hand.

2. Make a complete circle in front.

3. When the ball passes your right foot, give a small push upward.

4. When the baton is coming down, keep your eyes on the center of the shaft.

5. As the baton comes down just a little above the head, reach out with your right hand, palm out (knuckles toward you) and grasp the baton in the center.

Helpful Hints: Start out with "soft" aerials or aerials which you throw gently upward. *Practice keeping your eyes on the center of your baton. This is very important! Never take your eyes off your baton until it is caught.* From your "soft" aerials, work up to aerials which you throw upward harder and higher.

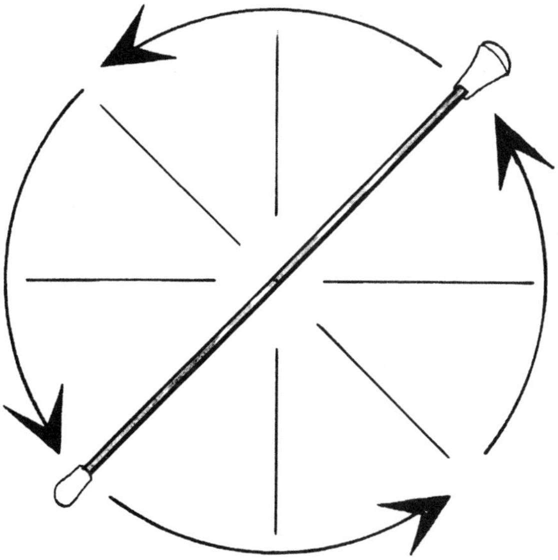

Time Toss – Catch Behind Back

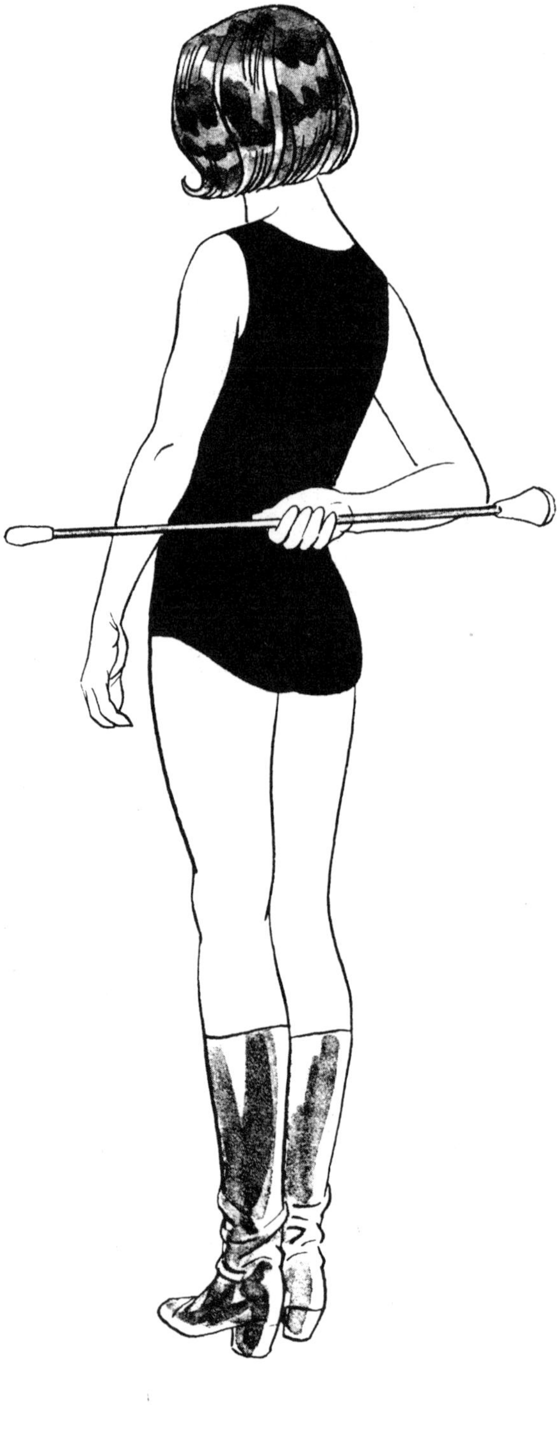

1. Hold baton in right hand (waist high) thumb to tip, knuckles will be up.

2. Begin a Time Toss, push baton upward a little above head.

3. Keep eyes on baton, turn quickly to your right and at the same time put right hand behind back to catch Time Toss as it is coming down.

Horizontal – Catch Behind Back

1. Hold baton thumb to ball in left hand. Do left hand horizontal twirls. While baton is still spinning in a horizontal twirl push baton upward high over head.

2. Quickly put right hand behind back and turn to your right looking over left shoulder so you can keep your eyes on your baton.

3. Bend head downward and catch in right hand behind back.

Time Toss – High in Front

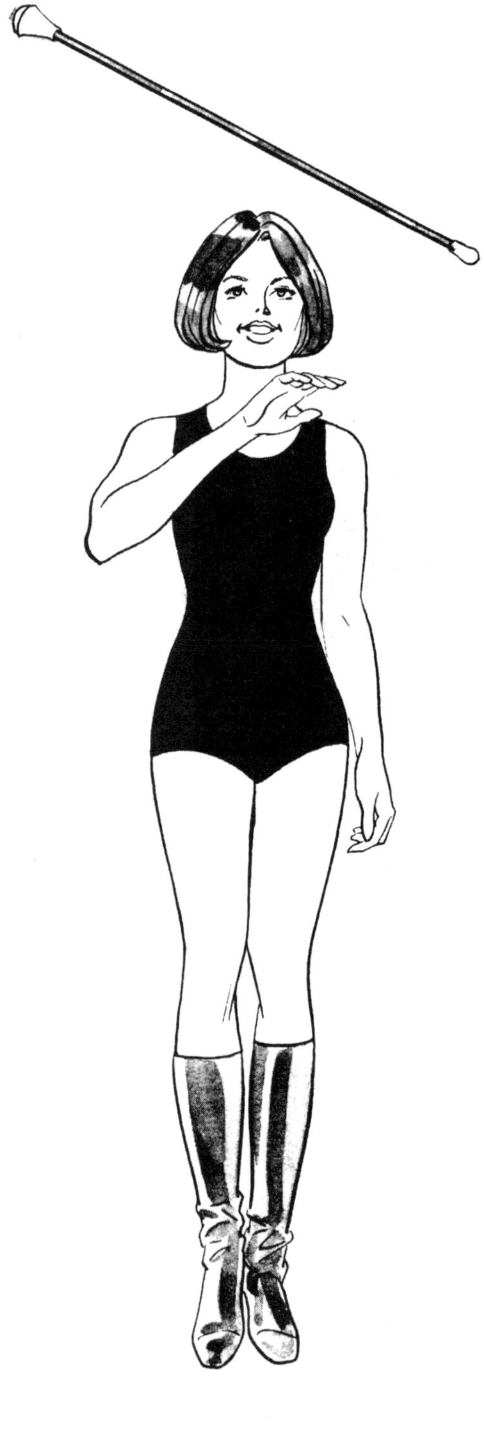

1. Do a Time Toss, raise right hand just as baton rolls off thumb.

2. When the baton is coming down, keep your eyes on the center of the shaft. When the baton is just above the head, reach out with your right hand, palm out (knuckles toward you) and grasp the baton in the center.

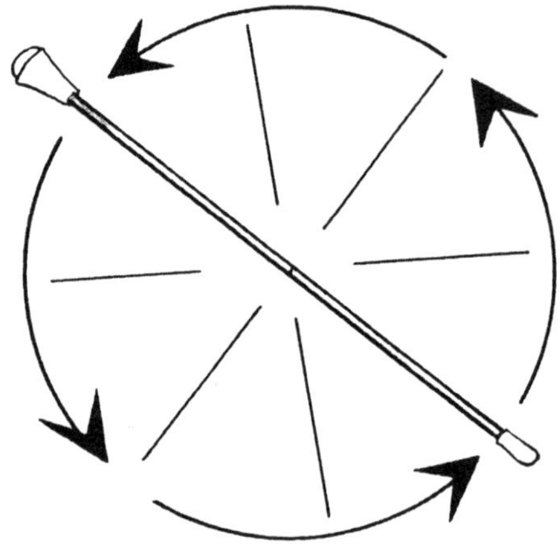

FLASH SERIES

Flash Leg-Pull Out

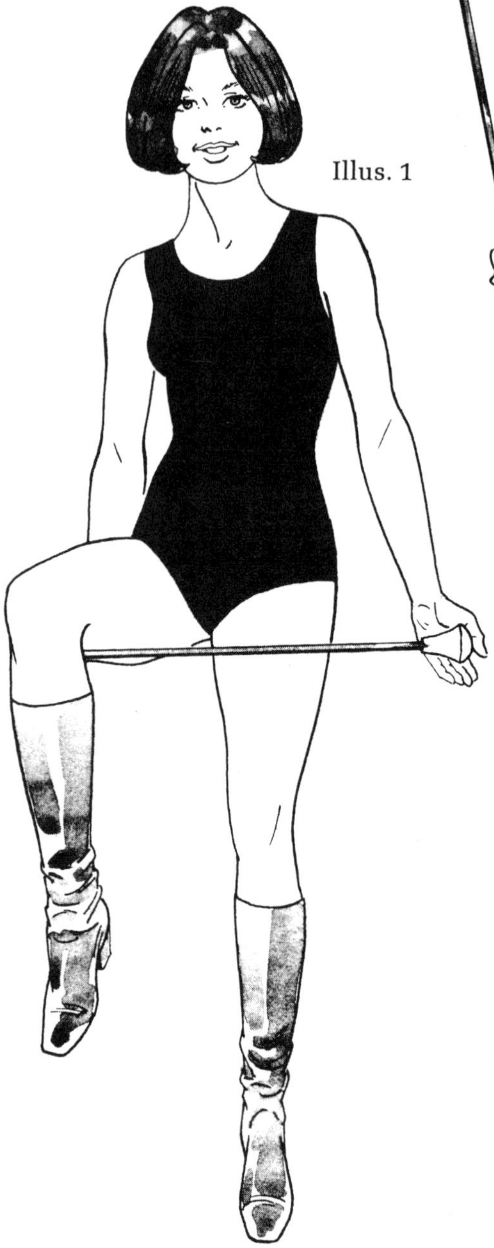

Illus. 1

Illus. 2

1. Hold baton by tip, thumb pointing towards ball of baton. (Illustration 1)

2. Bring baton under right knee. Be sure to point toe downward. (Illustration 2).

3. Bring right leg with baton pressed against it to your extreme right. Make sure your toe is still pointed. (Illustration 3).

4. Pull baton out when you get to right side, (Illustration 4).

5. End with your feet together, (Illustration 5).

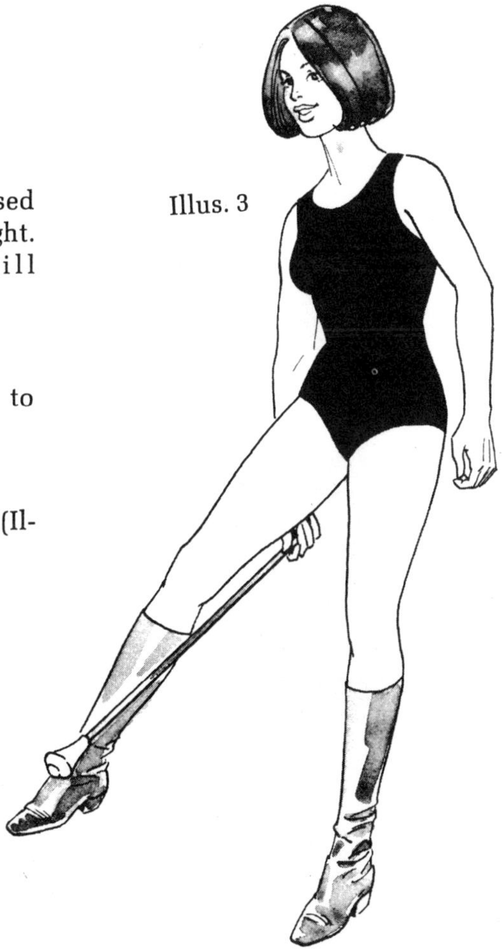

Illus. 3

Illus. 4

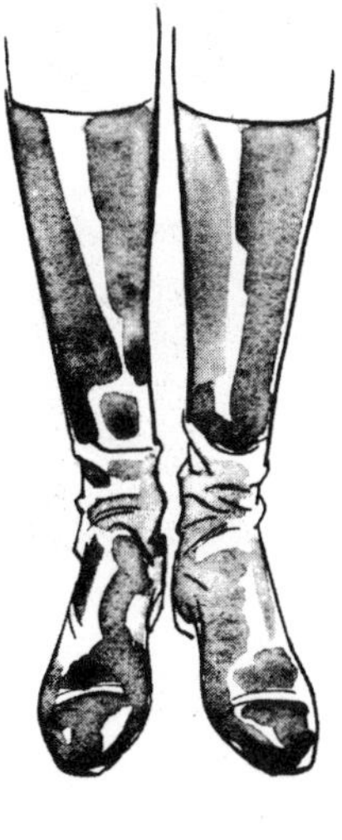

Illus. 5

Flash Ankle Flip

Illus. 1

1. Hold baton by the tip, thumb to ball, (Illustration 1).

2. Drop baton behind, (Illustration 2).

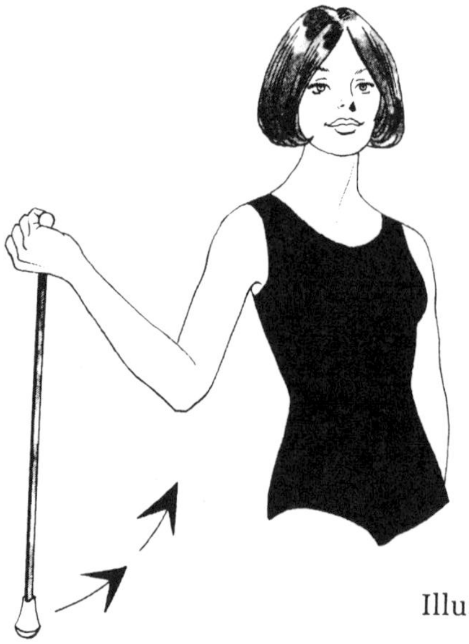

Illus. 2

Illus. 3

3. Bring baton up, completing circle, (Illustration 3).

Illus. 4

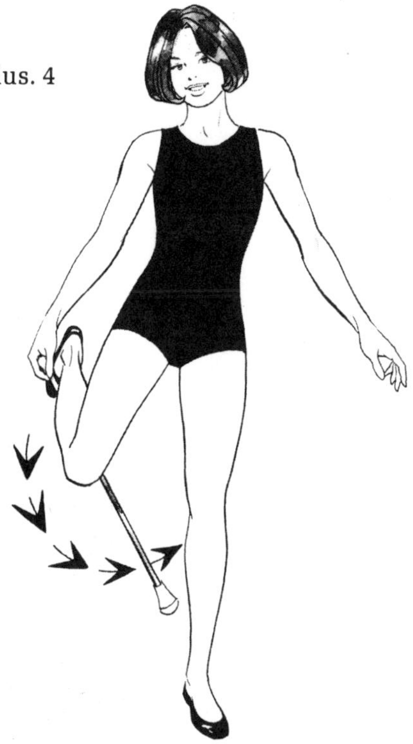

Illus. 5

Illus. 6

4. Bring right foot up. Bring baton under right ankle, (Illustration 4).

5. Baton will flip under ankle and make a complete circle, (Illustration 5).

6. Catch baton by ball, thumb to tip, (Illustration 6).

Leach Twirl

Illus. 1

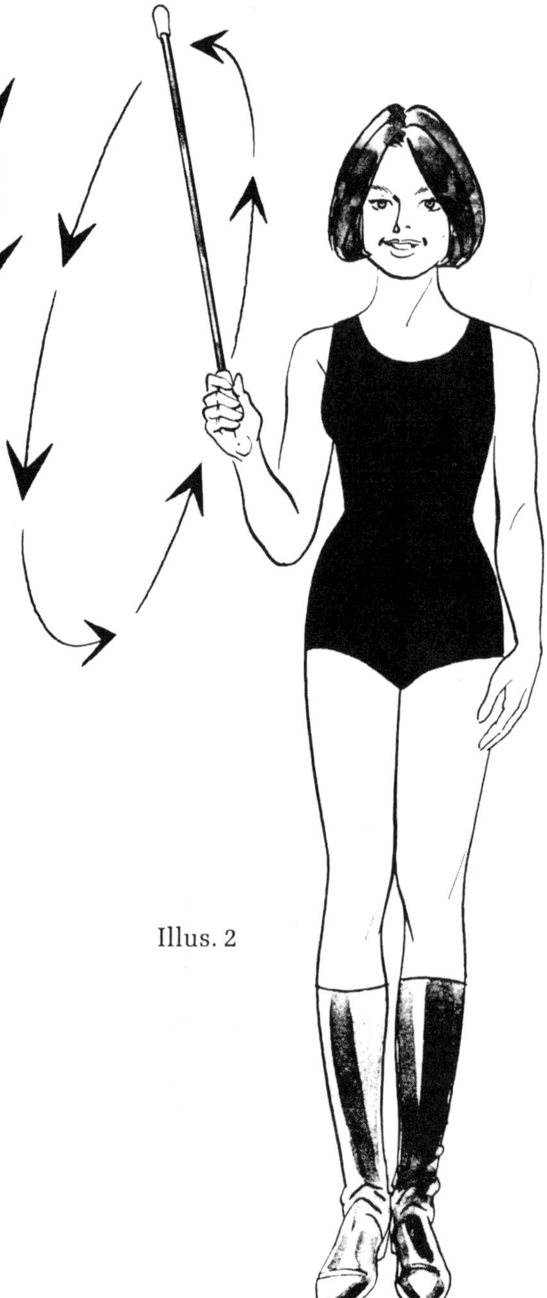

Illus. 2

1. Hold baton in right hand by ball.

2. Circle at left side in a forward circular motion. (Illustration 1).

3. Circle at right side in a forward circular motion. (Illustration 2).

4. Circle under left leg in a forward circular motion. (Illustration 3).

Illus. 3

Illus. 4

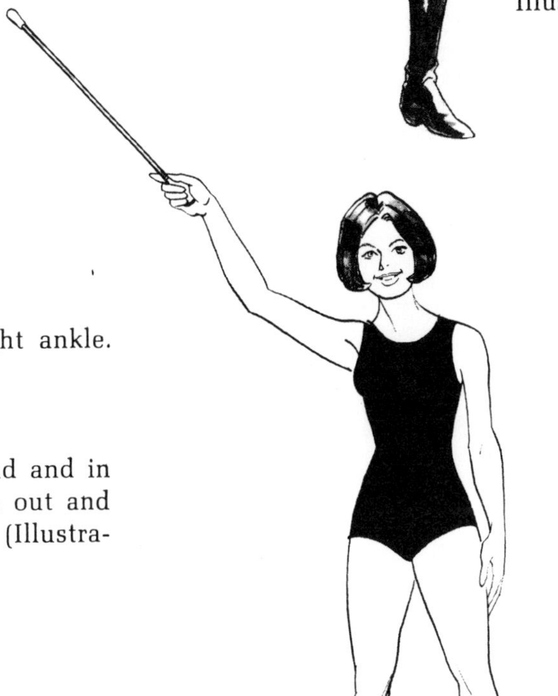

5. Bring baton around right ankle. (Illustration 4).

6. Hit baton with left hand and in one motion bring baton out and raise baton over head. (Illustration 5).

Illus. 5

(continued next page)

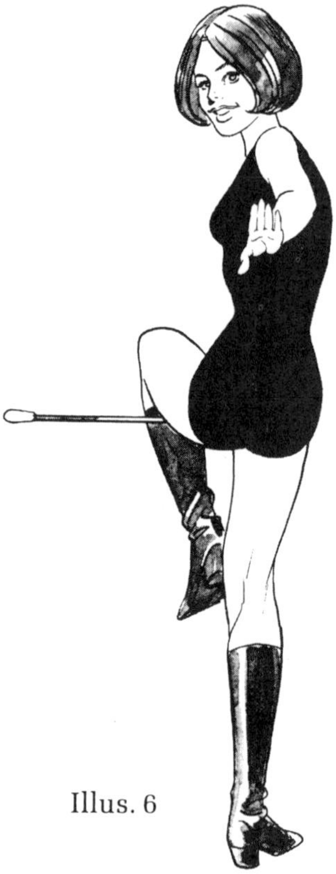

Illus. 6

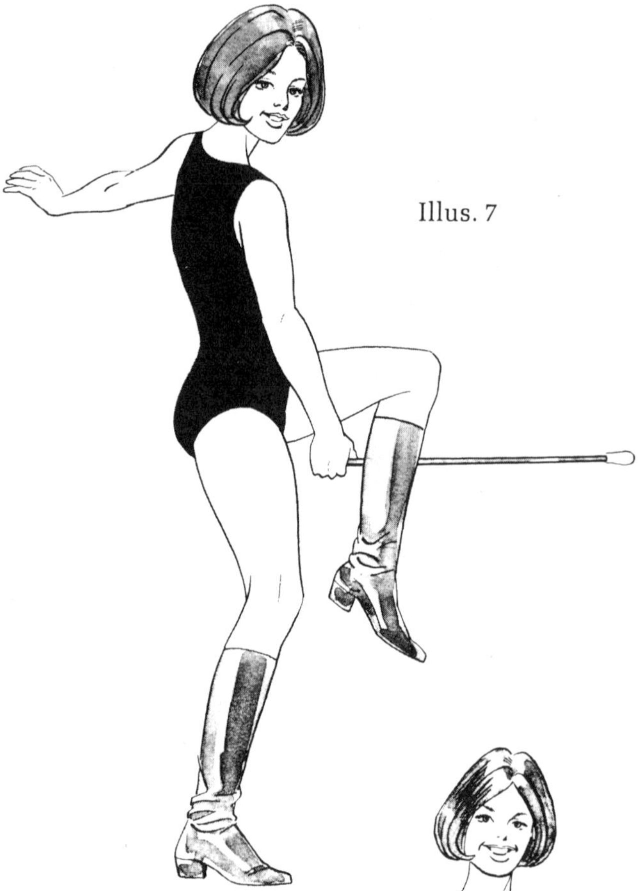

Illus. 7

7. Step down on right foot. Raise left knee, toe pointed downward.

8. Bring baton under left raised knee. (Illustration 6).

9. Swivel on the ball of your foot to your right. (Illustration 7). When you are facing the front then bring baton out. (Illustration 8).

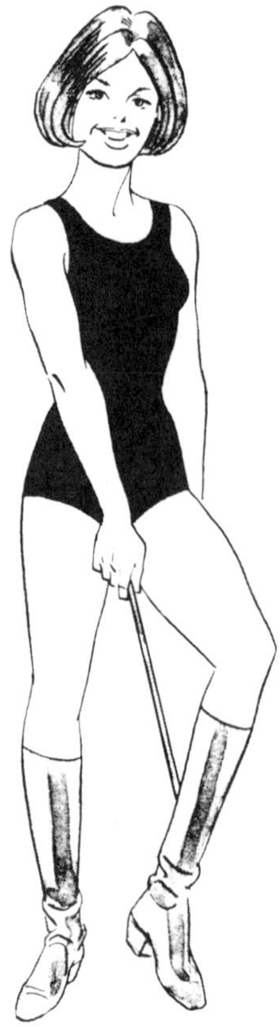

Illus. 8

Simple Flash

1. Do simple flash exactly as Leach Twirl 1, 2, 3 and 4.

2. Bring baton around right ankle, (Illustration 1).

3. Take in left hand to end twirl.

Illus. 1

More Advanced Flash

Illus. 1

1. Hold ball in right hand with left hand cupped over right hand. Circle on the left side to the back, (Illustration 1).

2. Circle in the middle to the right, (Illustration 2).

3. Circle on the right side, to the front, (Illustration 3).

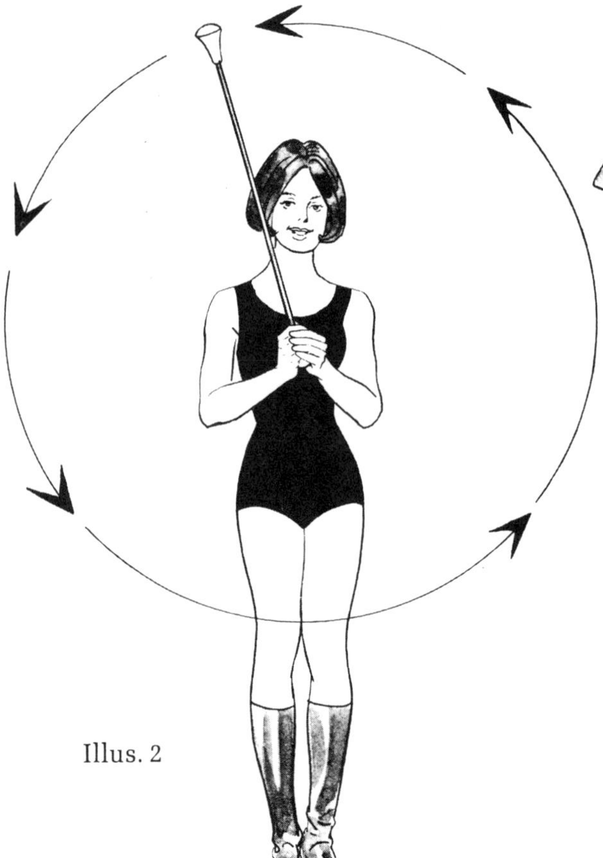

Illus. 2

Illus. 3

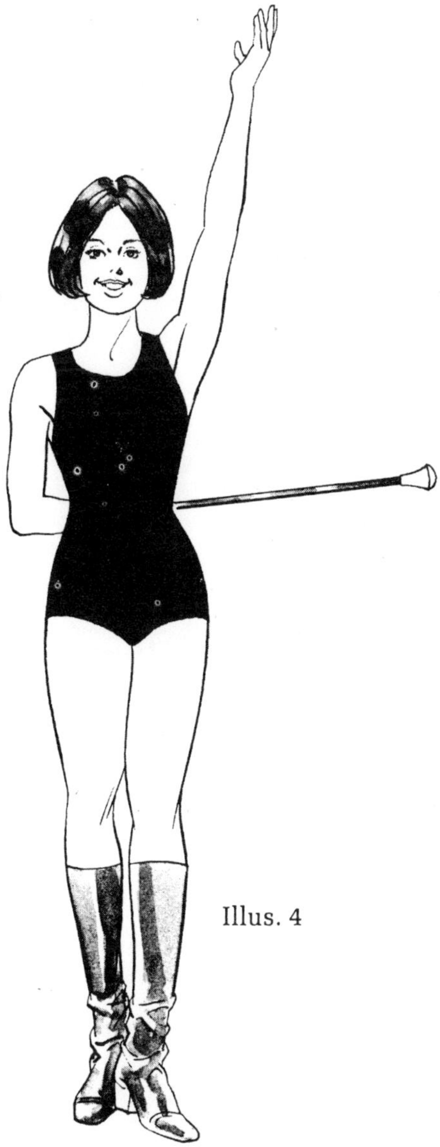

4. Remove left hand and bring it high in air, arm straight and fingers together. Bring baton which is in right hand to your back to the extreme left and touch left side to end twirl, (Illustration 4).

Illus. 4

MARCHING ROUTINES~ PARADE MARCHING

Marching Routines – Parade Marching

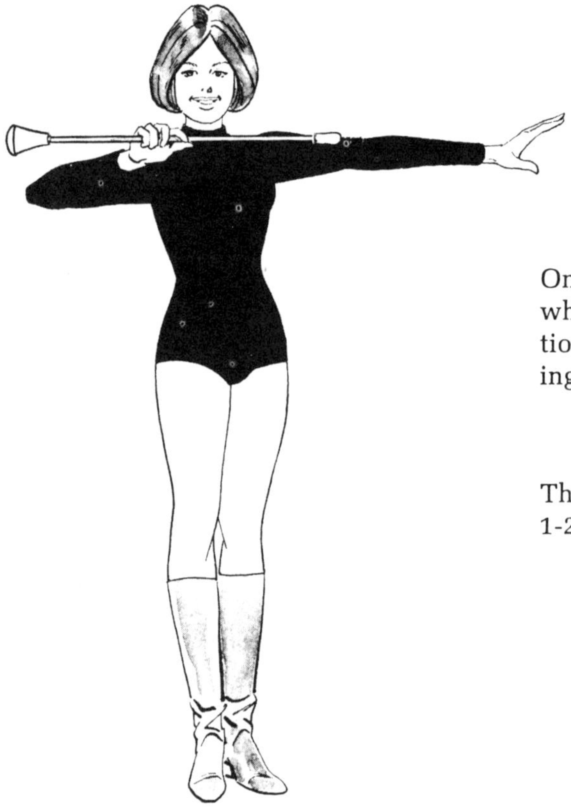

On the third tweet of the leader's whistle bring baton over to position in illustration while marching. Count 1-2-3-4.

Then over to the other side, count 1-2-3-4.

Repeat above procedure — left side 1-2-3-4, then right side 1-2-3-4.

Bring baton up on left side and do step, close step with feet.

Then over to other side and do step, close step with feet.

Repeat same above procedure on each side.

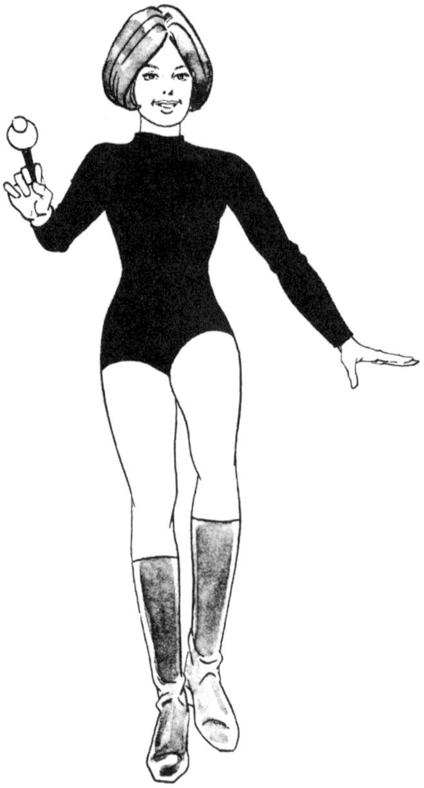

Then baton goes on arm and you march four steps, 1-2-3-4.

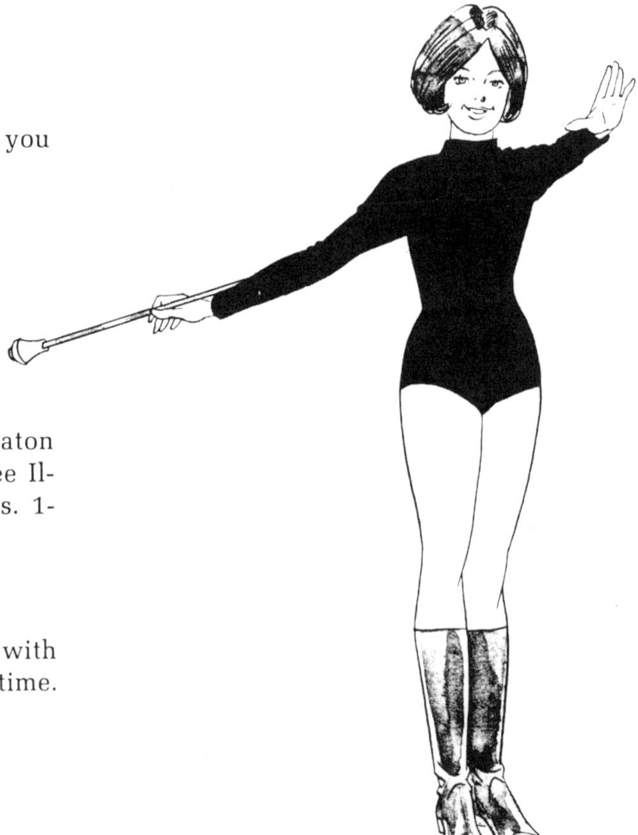

Stretch arms out. Arm with baton on it goes out front first. (See Illustration). March four steps. 1-2-3-4.

Stretch arms out again. Arm with baton on it goes in back this time. March four steps 1-2-3-4.

Holding baton near ball swing baton across front of waist to left side. Left arm goes straight up with hand flat. March four steps, 1-2-3-4.

Raise right arm with baton on it up and place left hand at waist and march four steps. 1-2-3-4.

Bring baton down to regular position on arm and finish routine by just marching with baton on arm.

Marching Routine 2

1. While marching, horizontal twirl in front (4 counts) March 1-2-3-4.

2. Horizontal in back, (4 counts) March 1-2-3-4.

3. Bring baton under elbows as in Illustration 1 and march four steps. March 1-2-3-4.

4. Take a step up and step kick as in Illustrations 2 and 3.

5. Baton rests on arm again to just march.

Illus. 1

Illus. 2

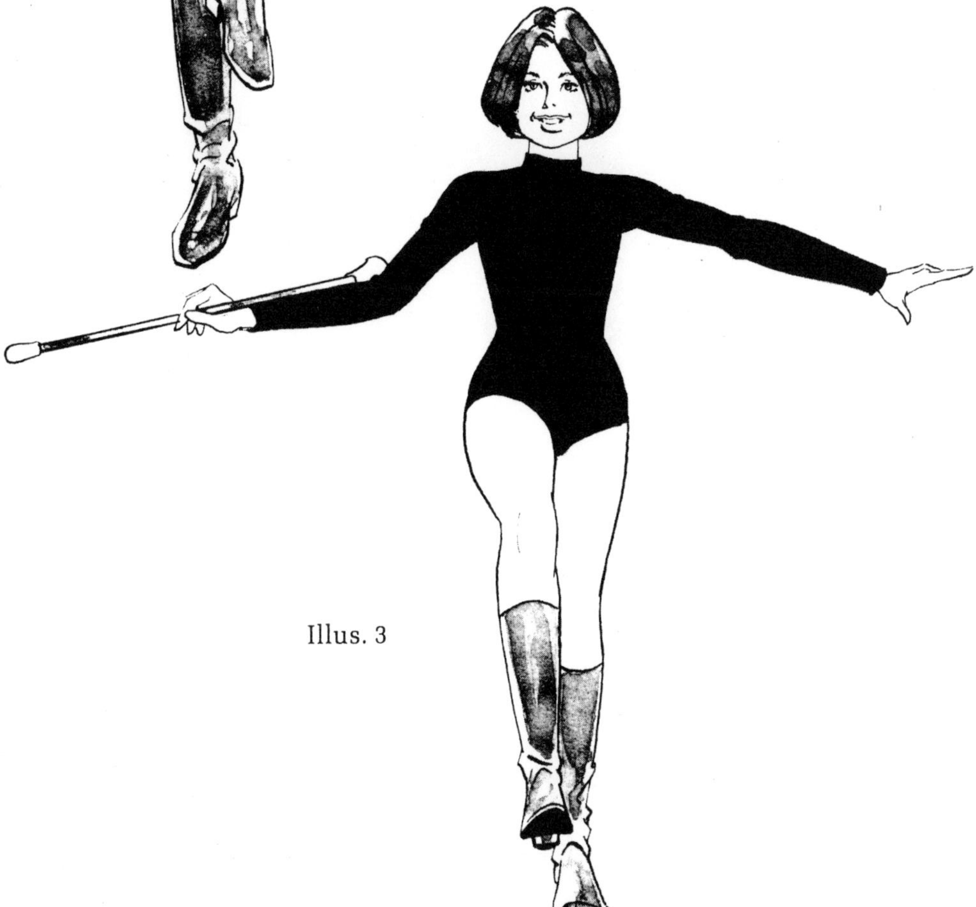

Illus. 3

How to Form A Parade Marching Team

If your school doesn't have a band or majorettes, why not form your own parade marching group. A group of 24 girls is an ideal number because the group will look large enough to be impressive. With 24 girls you can have the following:

Two flag bearers (1 American Flag & 1 State Flag)
1 Solo Twirler
2 Banner Carriers
1 Leader with a whistle
Marching/Twirling Group of 18

You would line up your girls up as follows:

```
     X     X        (Flag Carriers)

        X           (Solo Twirler)

X———————————X       (2 Banner Carriers)

        X           (Leader with whistle)

X       X       X
X       X       X
X       X       X
X       X       X
X       X       X
X       X       X
        O           (Drummer)
```

Don't despair if you don't have 24 girls. You can start with as few as 15 marchers and 1 leader with a whistle. You can have as many as you wish. I have one group which has 48 marchers.

The first thing you will need to do is secure enough interested girls who are slim and well groomed and are willing to work hard. The next step is to teach the group to march and twirl and train them to keep their rows straight across and back. Straight rows are very important. Some of the finest groups I have seen were new majorettes who kept their rows straight and had beautiful smiles on their faces.

The newly formed group will need to secure a baton instructor or a teenage advanced twirler to teach the group once or twice a week. The girls will need to be taught to march, and will need to learn their basic fundamentals and a snappy parade marching, twirling routine.

The leader of the group will need to be chosen and will lead the girls at each practice with the whistle. One tweet on the whistle will start the girls marching. Three long tweets on the whistle will signal the girls to begin the routine. The leader with the whistle will need to work out the signal to stop with the group. Our leader turns around to face the girls, marching backwards, with her baton in both hands over head and blows three short tweets. One tweet is blown with the baton extended high, the second tweet as she brings the baton down shoulder level and the last tweet as she brings the baton down waist level. The leader should practice the whistle signals enough with the marchers so that they will never be confused. They should be able to recognize readily the difference between three short tweets and three long tweets so they will know whether to begin the routine or stop.

The leader of the group will need to check with the local City Hall to find out the name of the person who is in charge of the parade scheduling. You will need to get acquainted with this person who schedules the parades so you can check with them fairly often to see which parades are coming up. Each parade will have a different parade marshal so always ask the name and how to reach that particular parade marshal.

You will need to have a name chosen for your group so you can give the parade marshal the name, number of girls and the telephone number or address where they can mail parade information. What you will need to know is the parade day, time of line-up, time of parade, place of line-up and where parade will end.

Once you have chosen a name for your group you will then need to make or buy a banner with the chosen name on it. We make ours from felt material because it is heavy and wide. We use two colors and cut out large letters to spell out our name and sew the letters on the long banner. Our banner measures 8′ x 2½′ and is on a long pole which is 9′ long. It is easily seen but a smaller banner is easier to carry. The choice is yours. The pole was purchased from a local lumber yard. The pole is a 1½″ dowell rod and costs around $3.00. Large ball fringe may be sewn on the bottom of the banner.

You will need two girls to carry the banner with the name on it. It is important that the banner girls march well and have a nice smile.

The first three rows should consist of your best marchers and twirlers so hold try-outs for these spots.

At the last marching practice before the parade make a chart showing where each girl is to march. Parade morning everyone is so nervous they will have difficulty remembering where they should be. Many of the brand new twirlers will be so excited and so uptight they won't even remember their own name. Muchless where they are to lineup.

Costumes, crowns and boots will need to be chosen. The costumes should be identical with the exception of the solo twirler. The solo twirler may have a costume of her own choosing and may have a different color costume as long as it looks well with the group's costume color.

Two very small girls may be chosen to carry the American Flag and the State Flag in the very front of the group. The girls should march well. The young flag carriers should be cautioned to never let the flag touch the ground. Small size flags are available which are ideal. The fabric area measures approximately 16½" x 11".

It is helpful to have a drummer to give the cadence so the girls will be able to stay in step. The drummer may be a boy or girl and should practice with the group at each marching practice. The drummer is positioned at the rear of the group and marches with the group during the parades.

If your group is not part of a school band when you are entering a parade ask to be placed either in front or in back of a band which plays music. It is so much more fun to march and twirl to music.

Tips for Parade Marching and Marching as Team

The most important advice that can be given to a group of majorettes is *practice together often.* Get to know each other. Care about each other. Help the twirlers that are having difficulty.

Set a fun goal for each twirling performance. If it is a parade the group is marching in, your goal could be to have the most smiling majorettes in the parade or you could set your goal to have the straightest lines in the parade or the best marchers in the parade. But it is important to strive as a group together to achieve a goal for that day.

It is very important to keep the rows straight. This will take practice and effort on each girl's part. It is important that the girl on the right keep the other two girls straight with her. The center marcher should watch constantly from the corner of her eye to make sure she is staying right with the girl on each side of her therefore keeping the row in perfect line.

A few helpful hints which my groups have tried and have found to be successful are the following:

- To keep the girls straight in their rows back and across I have tried to give the girls an incentive to stay straight by awarding first, second and third place ribbons to the straighest rows across and back. The blue, red and white ribbons I made from 1″ satin ribbon and gold large notary seals which I purchased at a stationery supply store. I cut the ribbon in 5″ long strips and stapled two at the top and stuck the notary seals, front and back, to make the award ribbon. From that day forth I never had to say a word to the rows. They kept each other so straight to win the ribbons that the expense of it was well worthwhile.
- Before we start off at the beginning of a parade I pass out hard lemon drops for the girls to keep their mouths from becoming so dry.
- During real cold parades we wear thermo underwear under our costumes and seamless panty hose on our legs to keep our legs warm and to also give them a nice tanned look.
- Parade Prize Money — The group should decide ahead of time what to do with the parade prize money that could be won by a sharp marching group. If it is split up it would give each girl so very little that our group decided to use whatever we won to do something for others. We purchase porch swings for our

favorite elderly people in our town. A little engraved plate can be glued on the back that says first prize won at so and so parade. This way our trophy will be enjoyed and used every day. It also makes the girls very happy to do something for others.

Solo Twirling with Parade Groups

Your very best twirler should be your solo twirler. The girls should be told in advance that a solo will be chosen. Ask the girls to put together a twirling/marching routine that she would use in the parade if she were chosen solo. The girl chosen should march well, be well groomed and wear a ready smile. Her routine should be showy and entertaining. The solo twirlers should work extra hours on her solo parade routine and be able to perform unafraid, marching well and head held high. The solo should do her routine often or the crowd will feel cheated.

How do you choose your solo. Let the group of girls help you judge. Stress that the girls should not vote for their friend but pick the best girl that is trying out so the group will be represented well. The girl picked should be the best overall girl—twirling ability, marching ability and personality. Pick the solo and an alternate in case of illness.

The solo can wear the group costume or a costume completely different even in color as long as it looks good with the group's costume color.

She can wear a crown or tiara on her head to show she is the solo.

The solo twirler will be a little nervous but she must realize she has an obligation to entertain. The crowds are watching her every move so she should be well prepared and ready to put on a good show whether it be strutting, smiling or doing her twirling routine.

MISCELLANEOUS

Smile - Smile - Smile

When a beginner twirler starts practicing her first fundamental twirls she should start practicing her smile. A beautiful smile is a must with a performing majorette. A smile can win your audience when you are twirling on stage and a smile when you are marching down the street will win you many smiles in return from the crowds of people along the way. A smile is of no value until it is given away. So give away that smile and enjoy doing it!

Your first parade will be your supreme test for smiling because you will be nervous and will be concentrating on your routine. Let me tell you a little secret: Most people do not know the difference between the hard twirls and the easy twirls. People are watching the over-all picture of you marching, smiling and performing. They merely judge by if you drop your baton if you are a good or bad twirler. The secret is to have a simple routine — one which you can do in your sleep! By knowing the routine well it will give you great confidence when you are performing. You know your routine well so march down the street proudly, strutting and smiling and loving every minute of it. If you are enjoying what you are doing it will show and the crowds will love it. *Showmanship* is the important thing on parade day.

Eye contact with the audience is very important also whether it be the crowds of people along the parade route or the people you can't quite see on the last row when you are twirling on stage or the judges on the reviewing stand. Look the people right in the eye and smile. Make them feel they are with you. It will give you a sparkle and help you to be an outstanding performer. Watch the performers that glisten and glow and you will realize this is their secret — eye contact with their audience.

Your Feet are so Important

Powder your feet well, especially between your toes before putting on your anklets or hose. Powder inside your boots or tennis shoes. Let inside of your boots or shoes dry thoroughly after each use so that the bacteria will not multiply. If you have a small fan let it blow on them to completely dry the inside.

Before the arrival of the parade season with the marching practices and long parades, you should toughen up your feet by going barefooted or by applying tincture of iodine once a week to the bottom and sides of your feet.

Many athletes wear two pairs of socks. Use a cotton sock next to your skin and a wool sock over the cotton sock so there will not be much rub to the skin to produce the blisters.

If you get a blister, it should be kept clean and dry and exposed to the air as much as possible. Watch carefully for any red streak traveling from the blister area because this could be a telltale sign of blood poisoning and you should see your doctor at once. Also if your blister should break or rupture you should see your doctor because this would be considered an open wound.

Miscellaneous Helpful Hints

1. Sweaty Hands — Sometimes during the excitement of your parades and twirling events your hands may get very moist. You can powder them just before going on and this will remedy this. You can fix your own palm duster by cutting a square from an old diaper and putting the powder inside and tying a string around it.

2. Tennis Shoes — If you want to keep your tennis shoes spotless until time for you to perform you can put large baggies over your shoes and use a rubber band around your ankle to hold the baggie on.

3. How to measure a baton. Extend arm straight out and measure from top of shoulder to tip of longest finger.

4. When purchasing a lighted baton or a fire baton choose one a good deal longer than your usual baton. Your beautiful circles of light or fire will be much more visible with a longer baton.

YOUR OWN NOTES

YOUR OWN NOTES

YOUR OWN NOTES

YOUR OWN NOTES